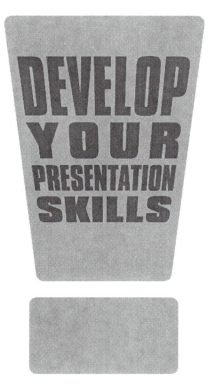

DEVELOP YOUR PRESENTATION SKILLS

THEO THEOBALD

CREATING SUCCESS

KoganPage

Publisher's note

Every possible effort has been made to ensure that the information contained in this book is accurate at the time of going to press, and the publishers and author cannot accept responsibility for any errors or omissions, however caused. No responsibility for loss or damage occasioned to any person acting, or refraining from action, as a result of the material in this publication can be accepted by the editor, the publisher or the author.

First published in 2011 by Kogan Page Limited
Second edition 2013

Apart from any fair dealing for the purposes of research or private study, or criticism or review, as permitted under the Copyright, Designs and Patents Act 1988, this publication may only be reproduced, stored or transmitted, in any form or by any means, with the prior permission in writing of the publishers, or in the case of reprographic reproduction in accordance with the terms and licences issued by the CLA. Enquiries concerning reproduction outside these terms should be sent to the publishers at the undermentioned addresses:

120 Pentonville Road	1518 Walnut Street, Suite 1100	4737/23 Ansari Road
London N1 9JN	Philadelphia PA 19102	Daryaganj
United Kingdom	USA	New Delhi 110002
www.koganpage.com		India

© Theo Theobald, 2011, 2013

The right of Theo Theobald to be identified as the author of this work has been asserted by him in accordance with the Copyright, Designs and Patents Act 1988.

ISBN   978 0 7494 6702 9
E-ISBN   978 0 7494 6703 6

British Library Cataloguing-in-Publication Data

A CIP record for this book is available from the British Library.

Library of Congress Cataloging-in-Publication Data

Theobald, Theo, 1957-
    Develop your presentation skills / Theo Theobald. – Second edition.
        pages cm
    ISBN 978-0-7494-6702-9 – ISBN (invalid) 978-0-7494-6703-6 (ebk.)   1. Business presentations.   2. Business communication.   I. Title.
    HF5718.22.T455 2013
    658.4′52–dc23   2012045515

Typeset by Graphicraft Limited, Hong Kong
Printed and bound by CPI Group (UK) Ltd, Croydon, CR0 4YY

CONTENTS

It's time to write... now! 32

The power of storytelling 43

Using humour 51

Progress report 159

What next? 165

PREFACE

We all want to be great presenters, but often for very different reasons. Some seek greatness on the world's political stage, others have more modest ambitions, possibly to be able to speak competently at the next company conference.

Maybe, what most of us want more than anything, is to avoid being a bad presenter. That's the category I'm in. For me there are two sides to this, the coach and the performer. Oh yes, I know what makes a great presenter, I can spot the flaws in anyone's delivery, give the presenter hints and tips to up his or her game, but somehow it's not so easy when you're trying to do it yourself – still, it doesn't stop me trying.

If you've ever had the slightest brush with the fine art of public speaking, some of what you read here will come as no surprise to you. This book looks at conquering nerves, how to use your voice, and good writing and rehearsal technique, to name but a few areas.

However, this is a discipline where 'experiential' learning is the key thing; 'learning by doing'. It's one thing sitting and reading about how to control your nerves, another entirely attempting to do it in a pressurized situation. So, the key to future success is going to be partly about the study of technique, but also about applying what you've learned in a real situation. The third, and arguably most important, part of developing your speaking skills, will be reflection – the chance to look back at your performance. There is an entire section dedicated to collecting both objective and subjective feedback on how you are progressing, to help you plan your future learning.

How would you rate your current skill level as a presenter? The truth is you're probably already much better than you perceive. You can think for yourself and conduct a conversation with another human being and that's all there is to it. They are the key attributes of an excellent performer. Now all you need to do is remember a few simple rules, get lots of practice and conquer your nerves.

Good luck, although with the right level of preparation you're unlikely to need it.

ACKNOWLEDGEMENTS

My thanks go to the Theo clan, all of whom are endlessly supportive when I'm researching and writing; they're the sort of people you'd want in your audience. To Kim, for her tireless efforts in editing and punctuation, plus all the encouragement from the sidelines. To Angie, for letting me steal her best ideas, not just for this, but for everything I do! To Laurence for being Laurence and furnishing me with the best story in the book. And finally, to Helen, for putting her faith in me yet again and sustaining our professional relationship, through thick and thin.

INTRODUCTION

There are dozens of books you could have chosen to improve your presentation skills, but this is the right one. So, there you have it – the first, and most important, rule of becoming a consummate presenter: confidence. Or, and this is the really critical bit, the *appearance* of confidence. No one need ever know if you are shaking inside, if you are terrified of your audience or mortified at the thought of making a gaffe; as long as you appear to be in control you will always look professional.

I hope that by following some of the advice here, which is based on long personal experience, both good and bad, and many, many conversations with business speakers and professionals from the stage, you give yourself the chance to be the best you possibly can.

Powerful presentations are a matter of two things, internal and external factors; the first is all about you, the unique package of DNA, experience, upbringing and environment that sets you apart from every other being on the planet. Whatever else you learn, either by reading this, by practising your presentations or by taking feedback from others, the most important thing of all when you are up there on the stage is to be yourself.

Aside from you, there are the 'external factors'. I would define these as the nuts and bolts of presenting, the things you can learn, practise and master; they include everything from writing and rehearsing your script, through to ensuring that you are introduced properly, weighing up the dynamics of the room and relying on the tools of the trade, from microphones to PowerPoint.

Combining the two sets of parameters together is what will help you achieve your 'personal best': a presentation that people will be talking about for a long time afterwards, for all the right reasons!

Before you jump in and start trying out new techniques, I hope that a bit of my own personal experience might help you. Right from the early days of doing presentations, I always wanted to be good at it, so I read many books, watched great speakers, noted what they did well and tried to incorporate it into my 'act'. I also listened to mentors, who would gladly offer advice on the best way to improve.

The downside of this is that I would stand up to speak with far too many thoughts running through my head: don't forget to smile, watch your body language, stop moving around the stage, slow your pace down, allow a bit of rise and fall in your voice and on and on. The truth is, I was so nervous that it was impossible to think of all these things at once.

So, what I would say to you, if you are still on an upward learning curve of speech making, is just concentrate on getting through it. Ensure that you know the content of your presentation as well as you can and use your instincts to deliver it in the best way you think fit. The more practice you get, the more able you will be to start thinking about some of the more advanced techniques. For now, congratulate yourself on having had the skill and resilience to get up and speak in public.

The chapters that follow are in rough chronological order, inasmuch as you have to write your presentation before you rehearse. In order to consolidate the learning of each chapter, there is a short, optional activity at the end for you to try out, along with a summary, in bullet point form, of what you have just read. If there is a particular area of expertise that you are trying to master, it might be worth revisiting the relevant chapter summaries when you are next in the process of preparing to speak.

If you are still not sure of where to start with brushing up on your skills, use the sorting grid overleaf (Figure 0.1) to decide on your priorities. Consider all the elements of making speeches, including:

- presentation skills;

- writing;

- rehearsal;

- use of voice;

- appearance of confidence;

- using autocue;

- visual aids;

- developing PowerPoint skills;

- assembling the right kit;

- finding low-risk opportunities to practise;

- humour;

- storytelling;

- handling nerves;

- handling an audience.

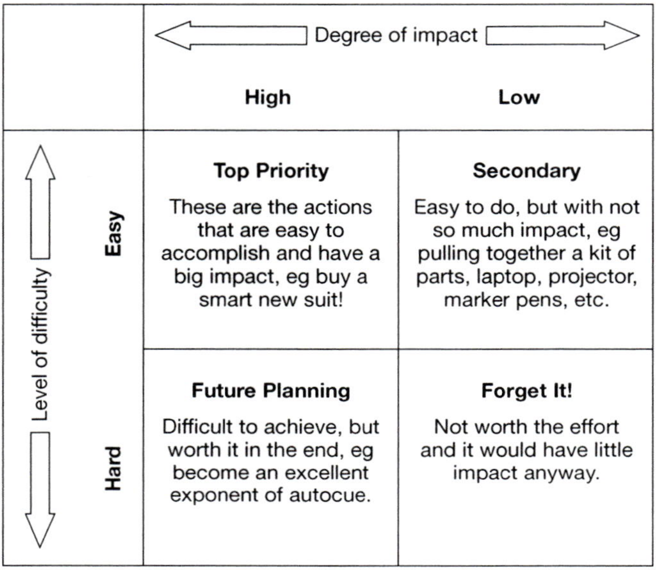

	Degree of impact	
	High	**Low**
Easy	**Top Priority** These are the actions that are easy to accomplish and have a big impact, eg buy a smart new suit!	**Secondary** Easy to do, but with not so much impact, eg pulling together a kit of parts, laptop, projector, marker pens, etc.
Hard	**Future Planning** Difficult to achieve, but worth it in the end, eg become an excellent exponent of autocue.	**Forget It!** Not worth the effort and it would have little impact anyway.

(Left axis: Level of difficulty)

Figure 0.1 Sorting grid for presentation skills

WHAT'S YOUR MOTIVATION?

In this chapter, we will look at the reasons why you want to improve your presentation skills, before taking time to think about who you are. What personal attributes do you already possess that will make you an even better presenter?

Very often we launch off on developing a new skill with only a vague reason why. It might be that you are increasingly called upon to stand up and deliver in front of an audience because of your job role, or perhaps you have seen and admired presentations given by a professional at work and that has made you aspire to be better.

If reinforcement of your decision were needed, below is a list of really good reasons to be a great presenter:

- Life is competitive and if you are going to succeed you will need to develop the skills of influencing and persuasion, so that your ideas get heard and adopted. The best way to do this is face to face and presentations allow you the opportunity to 'persuade' a large group all at once.

- The confidence gained from being a good public speaker can be translated into other areas of your business or personal life. Acquiring the skills of building effective arguments and delivering them well is likely to come in handy, even in small meetings, where you will be perceived as articulate and professional.

- Presenting well is enjoyable. It is one thing to have good ideas and innovative solutions, but the ability to convey these to a wider audience is a much more difficult skill set. When you manage to do it well, there is a great feeling of satisfaction. You might even get a round of applause!

- Good presenters are often seen as having more authority than their peers. Being asked by the MD to host the next conference will do your profile and career prospects no end of good.

- 'Entertainers' tend to be well liked. I am not advocating that this is the start of your stage career, but employing the right set of 'stage skills' will help to win you friends in business and beyond.

- The best ideas can get left on the shelf. If we don't have the gift of being able to present effectively, our frustrations may grow as our voice gets lost in the wilderness. It is one thing to develop a killer strategy, another entirely to get it adopted.

- Risk is a part of what all of us do and there can often be a direct correlation with reward. Presenting to an audience allows us the facility to take risks on our own terms and it is something we can build on, as our confidence grows.

- The skill of being a great presenter will always look good on your curriculum vitae (CV) or resumé. The same attributes will also help you outline your ideas and enthusiasm at a job interview.

- Challenge and resilience are a necessary part of achieving your goals, so overcoming nerves and speaking with confidence in public will give you practice of core skills.

- Planning and preparation, so necessary for effective management, are the most important parts of an excellent presentation; they will provide another string to your bow.

So, there are many benefits, both business and social, to being 'good on your feet'. Getting that way is not as difficult as you might think.

PERSONAL GOAL SETTING

Having decided that you want to improve your speaking technique, it is time to be honest and think about how much. The list of great modern orators includes Tony Blair, Bill Clinton, Martin Luther King, Nelson Mandela and Barack Obama – all leaders of one sort or another on the world stage.

We can learn a lot from studying these people and the techniques they use, but we cannot *be* them, we can only be ourselves. And here is the most important point of this whole book; the title has been carefully chosen as *Develop Your Presentation Skills*. It is about maximizing *your* personal potential, making you the best you can possibly be. So set your expectations realistically; don't try to become the people you admire, just learn from them and adapt your new knowledge to enhance your own presentation persona.

THE PRESENTER'S ALTER-EGO

Up there on stage, many of the best presenters appear to be 'larger than life'. If you meet them afterwards, they are most likely very much the same as the person you have just witnessed, but then they return to their 'normal' selves again. One of the reasons for this is that they are 'putting on a performance' when they present. Their gestures appear bigger and their passion greater because they have recognized that in order to get their message across effectively, they need to exaggerate themselves a little.

I am not suggesting that it is a conscious process, but it seems as if they have the ability to create an alter-ego, literally an alternative version of themselves, who gets up and does the hard work on their behalf. This can be a very helpful technique when attempting to overcome nerves and deliver a big presentation. In a sense, it is the more confident, outgoing, risk-taking side of our character that comes to the fore.

Good idea

We all have a little of the Jekyll and Hyde about us in that we are able to adapt to the social circumstances we are in, so even when we are not feeling particularly confident inside we can 'front up' a side of our personality that will make us appear, to the watching audience, to be more so. This is the part of you that will look best and deliver well, so before you set foot on the speaker's platform, hand the responsibility for the presentation to your personal, self-assured Mr Hyde.

The tools and techniques your alternative self will use are explained as we go through the chapters, but these are only of any use when allied to you, the speaker.

WHO ARE YOU?

No, really, it's a serious question. What do people see when they meet you?

An entire industry has grown up in recent years around the topic of emotional intelligence (the softer 'people' skills) that great leaders use, as a matter of course. One of the foundation stones of these principles is that of self-awareness and it is really important when you are making a speech.

Perhaps you have been in a situation at some point in your life when someone has told you about a perception that has taken you by surprise. Maybe a good friend has said 'When I first met you, I thought you were a bit stand-offish.' This could, for example, have been a simple misinterpretation of your 'shyness' on that person's part. Whatever the cause, the outcome is the same.

The big question is: 'Can we influence the way we are perceived by an audience, when we stand up to speak?' The answer is only a 'yes' if we take the time in advance to think about the main factors that might affect this. Being realistic about where we are now and setting some improvement targets helps our self-awareness, which ultimately should improve our overall performance.

All of these topics are covered in much greater detail shortly, but at this early stage it is worth briefly considering the main elements of character that we might want to build upon, with particular regard to making speeches.

MAIN ELEMENTS OF CHARACTER

Passion

We are all passionate about something; each one of us has pet subjects that we get fired up about, even if it is utility companies with multiple-choice telephone menus or the lack of respect among today's teenagers! D H Lawrence once said, 'Be still when you have nothing to say; when genuine passion moves you, say what you've got to say, and say it hot.'

The big question here is how prepared you are to let your passion show. The old British way of 'stiff upper lip' tends to suppress a lot of the natural passion of the nation. In the United States there is much more freedom for both men and women to express their feelings, in private life, in business and in making speeches.

One thing is certain: audiences like to see passion from their host. It is an admirable quality when harnessed in the right direction, so showing a will to win, a desire to overcome injustice or a longing simply to make things better will always score great points for you. Passion is hard to practise and even harder to fake, but if you write material that you feel passionate about, your feelings will follow when you are presenting.

Wit

Are you quick-witted – either in the sense that you can instantly spot the funny side of a situation, or that you are bright, have your 'wits' about you and can respond to adversity? Both of these definitions are useful assets in the presentation arena. Even when you are meticulously prepared, things can, and often do, go wrong.

If you are able to show the members of an audience that you are unfazed by such events, you will win their hearts. A speaker who can rescue the situation when the PowerPoint fails, rather than stomping off the stage in a hissy fit, will definitely make friends and influence people.

Equally, if you are able to crack a joke in response to something that has just happened in the room, you will also endear yourself. This can be especially true if you have a question and answer session at the end of your address. Incidentally, such humour can be very valuable in diluting a potentially aggressive round of questioning. If the audience members hear what the 'heckler' has to say and sees you deal with it, they will be on your side.

Professionalism

This is a word that covers a multitude of topics. What do you think professionalism looks like in a presenter? Some aspects are seen in presenters who:

* turn up in plenty of time;

* are unflustered by anything that is thrown at them and takes things in their stride;

* look the part – are smartly dressed, look alert and are smiling and confident;

* have all the 'assets' of their presentation (slides, script, props, etc) to hand.

Your list may well be longer than this, but what virtually all aspects of professionalism have in common is that they can be 'acquired' by pre-planning. Being alert is about having sufficient sleep the night before; smartness of dress relates to the attention to detail that makes sure your clothes fit, are clean and pressed, and your shoes have been shined. All of these little details count.

TIP

If you give all of this attention to detail before you get on stage, you are bound to exude a professional demeanour once you start to speak. This is a great credibility builder and audiences love it.

Expertise

Stick to your specialist subject area and you will look and sound confident. You don't necessarily have to spend 20 minutes focused on telling members of the audience why you are so knowledgeable on this topic, they will sense by your air of authority soon enough if you are the genuine article.

If you are talking on a subject you have limited knowledge of, just deliver what you have to and don't start trying to embellish the content with 'false expertise'. If you are forced into handling a question and answer session at the end of such a speech, find a form of words that lets those in the audience know you are not a topic expert, but if you cannot answer their queries right away, you have a team of specialists who will swing into action and get an answer back to them within a day or two.

Charisma

I have left charisma until last, because despite having studied and written about it extensively over many years, I am still not convinced it exists, at least not in isolation.

There are definitely individuals who we are drawn to, who are 'more attractive' than the average person – I don't mean physically – who we would sit up and take notice of if we heard them speaking. Is charisma something you can define in a logical way though, or is it too much of an emotional quality to do so? As I say, I am not sure of the answer to this one. What I do know is that if you combine all the factors above together, in one package, and add a pinch of your own natural personality, you will have a recipe for charisma, because I honestly believe it is something that can be developed by most of us, even if there are a few people we envy, who seem to have been born with it. I cannot help feeling that by developing your presentation skills you will develop a higher degree of charisma at the same time.

Activity

Think of a great public speaker, either a famous person whose presentation you haven't actually attended or someone you have watched and heard yourself. With the person in mind, draw up your own comprehensive list of the qualities he or she possesses. Try to make these one-word descriptions.

Give yourself a mark out of 10 for each quality, then think about how you could improve that score.

SUMMARY

● There are lots of great reasons to improve your presentation skills; take some time now and again to review these and remind yourself why you are doing this.

● You might admire other presenters and public speakers, but you cannot be them. It is much better to observe what they do and adapt it to your own personality.

● Be a bit larger than life when you are up there on stage, as it helps the audience get a sense of who you are.

● Understanding the person you are is part of improving yourself in the eyes of your audience.

● Consider some of the attributes of good speakers and think of how these apply to you.

WHERE DO YOU BEGIN?

Not all presentations are the same, so the amount of time and effort you put into preparing and delivering different presentations will vary. How do you keep all that in proportion? Let's have a look at that question, as well as thinking about what opportunities there are to go out and seek speaking engagements proactively.

The work you put into a speech or presentation will, most likely, not be governed by things like the size of the audience or the length of the address. It is much more likely that the importance of the occasion – such as your brother's wedding or a massive sales pitch – and who the audience is will be the deciding factors. Incidentally, this rule will also apply to how nervous you are likely to feel. Often, professional speakers will admit that they are more afraid of a forthcoming speech as best man at a wedding, in front of 50 intimate friends, than an hour-long conference address to an audience of 500.

DIFFERENT TYPES OF PRESENTATION

I have compiled some notes on the kinds of presentation you might be asked to deliver. These are designed to act as a quick guide, so that you can get the task into perspective and start to take some instant decisions about how you are going to prepare.

The family occasion

I have started with this one as it is the most personal kind of presentation we are called upon to do. It might be as formal as a wedding speech (say, as the father of the bride) or just a few well-chosen words on the occasion of grandma's 80th birthday.

As mentioned earlier, very often we are most nervous for this kind of speech, which is a paradox really, as we are presenting to an audience of people who are already firmly on our side. I have never seen an angry heckler at a wedding – an amusing one, yes.

Humour is, of course, appropriate. For example, in the case of grandma's birthday, who could resist recounting some of her more eccentric moments? However, these occasions are also a time for heartfelt sentiment and it is this bit that unnerves most of us, as we try to make sure we express what we feel and not mess it up. The advice here is to keep the emotional bit short, save it for the end, don't make it too slushy and rehearse it tirelessly until it comes out like you want it to.

You won't have to worry about PowerPoint or props for this one, though it is worth considering the physical space you are in. For the wedding you will have the room to yourself, but for the milestone birthday (or other such occasion) you might be in a restaurant, shared with other diners. In this case, try to negotiate a table that is tucked away, perhaps in its own alcove. Otherwise, be prepared for the wider world to hear your expressions of devotion!

Business – internal and informal

This category covers the most common type of presentation – the presentations you give to your peers or colleagues in your organization on an ongoing basis. Here you might expect an audience of up to 50 people and often the purpose will be to impart information and allow for some kind of discussion.

They won't be expecting you to do a full 'song and dance' routine; these are the people who know you well professionally, so you really need to be yourself. However, this does not excuse 'taking them for granted' and giving a below-par performance. Often, the thing that marks one person out for success, over another, is that person's passion and enthusiasm for the subject. Don't try to manufacture this, but look for the parts of the speech that stir you and show some emotion.

Usually you will have a high degree of control over the environment (the boardroom, or some other similar meeting space), so it won't be necessary to do a full check of the ergonomics of the surroundings. Technical issues shouldn't prove a problem either.

Keep in mind that the members of this audience will have a high degree of familiarity with the subject matter, so don't patronize them with unnecessary detail or bore them with facts they already know. Instead look for something new, some interpretation and analysis of what is currently happening.

Business – internal and formal

One example is where the boss kindly requests that you deliver a formal address at the annual conference for all staff. Even if you work in a small organization, there is a lot to be learned from preparing for this kind of speech. Let's say for now that the venue is still an internal one. You are familiar with the room set up, the necessary technology is all in place and you have access in advance for rehearsal. Most of these things are under your control.

Focus now on the content of what you are going to say, because it is likely to be scrutinized more closely by an audience of knowledgeable peers and colleagues, not to mention your boss. Although I always think it is a good idea to have a few surprises up your sleeve for the audience so as to engage better with them, this is a case where you will need to share the content of your address in some detail with other platform speakers, so that you neither duplicate nor contradict each other.

Business external

This category can cover anything from a sales pitch or presentation of your organization's credentials to you being asked to deliver a conference speech at another company's event.

Preparation for this needs to be top notch. You are representing your company and it is also a showcase for you as an individual.

The audience is likely to be polite and respectful – after all you are an invited guest – but don't let that make you complacent. Unlike the internal situations, where you are familiar with the surroundings and equipment, you will now have to put in extra effort to get a working knowledge of what you will be dealing with on someone else's patch. It might also be the case that a third-party venue, such as a hotel or conference centre, has been hired for the occasion. Either way, make sure you do the legwork to understand the technology and the ergonomics of the room, as well as obtaining a full briefing about the members of the audience and their expectations.

Guest speaker

This can be very like the category above, but I have used it in the context of a less formal kind of address, so you might have been asked to give a fairly light-hearted introduction to an event, to act as facilitator or deliver an after-dinner speech.

Shortly, we will look at making opportunities for practising making speeches, which will include volunteering to be guest speaker at local clubs and societies. Just because you are unpaid and the number of people in the audience is generally small, don't treat them with contempt. This is a great training ground, but only if you take it seriously.

If you can prepare some interesting content, you should be able to adapt it for a number of different events, which will help you with the skill of honing your material and give you a good understanding of the elements that work best for you.

Compere, comedian, clown

When you get to this level, it is because people recognize your skill in front of an audience. Fundraising and social events are usually crying out for a professional to grab them by the throat and make sure that the audience's expectations are managed, so that everybody has a good time.

Does your local design college have an end-of-year fashion show, or are organizers of an event at the dance academy looking for an expert to keep their things flowing along? All of these are opportunities to try something new, with skills that are very much transferrable to other aspects of your presentations.

You should be perceived as the laid back, confident, anchor man or woman, so guess what you will have to do? Yes that's right, give it lots of thought and prepare what you are going to say. Decide a strict running order with a contingency plan for when things inevitably go wrong. Just because an event is fairly informal, doesn't mean it should be uncontrolled – it is important to stop it degenerating into a shambles. As the person with the microphone, you can have a big influence over this.

These are just some examples. There are bound to be circumstances where you are asked to speak that are not covered here, but I hope there are enough general tips in broad categories for you to be able to pick and choose what will work best, according to the circumstances.

The important thing is to keep a sense of proportion, but still to treat every opportunity seriously. It is true that if you deliver a poorly prepared speech at the local photographic society, to an audience of 12, it is unlikely to have a devastating effect on your career. However, when you do badly, you instinctively know and it does have a lasting effect on your confidence. As confidence is the key to getting you through some difficult presentations, you need to nurture it, stay positive and avoid having it dented by poor preparation.

DESPERATELY SEEKING SPEAKING

Never stop improving on your presentation technique. I just cannot emphasize enough the need for practice – that's what really makes one speaker stand out from the next and if confidence building is what you are trying to achieve, what could be better than having lots of chances to try out your skills?

But where do you start? What opportunities are there to hone your skills? The answer is to start small and be proactive.

The reason I say 'start small' is that you are much more likely to be able to find small groups of people who will be happy to listen to you, rather than attempt an address at the Royal Albert Hall in London. The strange thing about audience size is that most speakers don't pay much attention to it once it gets above a certain number. 'Dying' on stage is just as horrible in front of 50 as 500 people, the difference is just that in the latter case there are more people who are able to relate the tale to their friends. At first, there is a kind of psychological fear that might increase in line with the size of the crowd, but soon enough you just get used to the fact that there are 'some' people out there; it could be a few or many.

Every town has its own collection of societies and clubs with special interests and their regular meetings can be much enlivened by the services of a willing, interesting and, most importantly, free speaker. Start by identifying what is going on around you. Are there women's interest groups that meet regularly, business or charitable societies, events that are based on hobbies, such as for photographers, gardeners or bird-watchers? Next, try to map your own interests and/or experiences to the things that might resonate with the group. What have you done in your life that makes a great story? How about a holiday when you went on safari, the time when you were part of a mountain rescue team or a Christmas break when you helped out in a soup kitchen for the homeless? It can be anything really, because it is not the topic that matters, but the opportunity to increase your presentation 'flying hours'.

Some groups will have a set format and will expect you to tie in with that, but most are fairly informal and are happy to go with what you suggest, as long as it is reasonable. Plan to present for around 20 to 30 minutes. Try to keep the content interesting. A 'show and tell', where you take some physical object with you that the audience can examine, is always a good idea. There is usually an expectation that you will finish with a question and answer session.

Always ask for feedback from your host after the event and add that person's opinion to your own feeling of what went well, or not so well. Use this information to help you improve.

Set a realistic target of, say, making one speech a month. It might mean that after a while you will need to start travelling to the next district, but often this happens anyway, as you are recommended by your first group to an adjacent one. Build up a file containing details of what you said to each group, when and where and also the contact details of the person at the society or club who booked you. When you have developed new material, you will be able to make a second approach and will be welcomed with open arms, if you delivered well in the first place. These are also the kind of people who might be prepared to give you a glowing testimonial when you are chasing future bookings.

Even closer to home there are occasions in most social circles when it is appropriate for someone to deliver what my old man used to call 'a few well-chosen words'. Engagements, big birthdays (especially those marking decades), milestone anniversaries and christenings are all the kind of occasion when people often appreciate someone marking it with a short speech, usually, in my experience, culminating in a toast. Your first priority here will be to perform the duty of proposing the toast, rather than practising techniques of eye contact or voice control, but never let an opportunity to be 'on your feet' slip by.

As your confidence grows, make sure you stay proactive in looking for opportunities to speak. Even a few sentences of welcome for a party of visitors to your company or an opportunity to act as host introducing other speakers at a business event will help to build up your 'flying hours'. In these early stages, it is a good idea to develop a bank of different topics to speak on. This will increase your chances of being asked to present and has the added benefit of giving you lots of practice at writing new material. However, also think hard about whether you have some unique experience that you could relate to a variety of different audiences – something so different from most people's everyday lives that it stands alone as a great story.

Activity

Spend 30 minutes tracking down a list of what's on in your locality. Think about the kind of societies mentioned in this chapter and use different sources, including local newspapers, an internet search or friends and neighbours to draw up a list. Choose the top three organizations that you think you could speak to and telephone them to find out their policy regarding speakers. Based on what you discover, map out a plan of action to secure a speaking engagement within the next month.

SUMMARY

- Make quick judgements about the sort of presentation you have been asked to do, so that you can put an appropriate amount of time and effort into it.

- Consider the importance of the speech to you, rather than just looking at the size of the audience or the prestige of the event.

- Actively seek out local opportunities to get you started on the speaker circuit, compile a file containing contact details and the requirements of each group.

- Keep as much variety in your content as possible. This will expose you to a much greater range of audiences.

- Stay alert to new opportunities, don't be a shrinking violet and be sure to volunteer for any speaking engagement you can.

3

WHAT ON EARTH ARE YOU GOING TO SAY?

When you are an aspiring speaker, you may see a presenter with the enviable ability to make what seems a spontaneous, unscripted speech, full of heartfelt sentiment, wit and articulate observation. The truth of the matter is that, mostly, it has been written and rehearsed in advance, giving it the appearance of being off the cuff. In this chapter we are going to start looking at a process to begin your writing, so that you can make the most of the new speaking opportunities you are seeking. It is sometimes difficult to know where to begin, so as a starting point here are some general rules.

START WITH THE AUDIENCE

Before you even think of putting pen to paper, you have to consider the most important people in this whole process: the members of the audience. However fascinating your subject matter is to you, the acid test is whether you engage the people you are delivering to. Nothing else matters as much.

With some presentations, such as an internal company one, you will be able to gauge the crowd accurately, because of your intimate knowledge of how the organization works and its culture. However, once you step out in the big wide world, you will be making guesses about who the members of the audience are and about their expectations. Contrast the attitudes and psyche contained in a room full of primary school teachers with those of the teenage children of city bankers. Although you could probably make some assumptions about both, you might be surprised by some of the realities. The lesson is, if possible, try to speak to a few of these people before you put pen to paper. If you can find out what their lives are like, their loves and hates, problems and passions, then you will find it much easier to write in a way that appeals to them.

In the absence of this kind of personal research, do your best to get hold of a delegate list in advance. At the very least, you will know the gender balance of the crowd. Sometimes, at business events, the job title of each delegate will appear on the list too, providing you with information about their seniority and the type of job they do. All of this is useful in compiling a picture of what they are like.

DEVELOP TEMPLATES

Everyone will tell you that no two presentations are the same and it is most definitely the case that we should do our best to take account of a different audience, the dynamics of a room, the mood and atmosphere. That said, having some standard material that can be adapted across a range of presentations is a good thing too.

Good idea

When you are writing, rehearsing and delivering your speeches, think about how different elements can be adapted for other presentations. Do you have a killer opening that, with a bit of thought, could be used on different occasions? A good example of this might be a generic story about yourself, or an issue that you feel passionate about – the environment, respect in society, the need for strong leadership, releasing people's potential (it's up to you) – which you can use as a lead in to whatever you have been asked to speak about.

The same is true of stories. Often, a good anecdote will stand alone and might easily be related to a range of topics that you are called upon to cover. A professional stand-up comedian once told me that he had only ever used a handful of opening lines in his entire career. He said, 'If you've used a line before and it's worked, you get attached to it, you don't want to let it go.'

If you think about a presentation structurally, say as a list of three major points you are going to talk about, then you can practise coming up with these across a variety of topics, so that when you get asked spontaneously to make the case for increased use of IT in our business (or any other topic), you will have a ready-made format you can use.

TOPICALITY

Being up to the minute with your topic is a great way of showing members of your audience how 'in touch' you are, with the added bonus that they are likely to have been concerned about the same thing themselves, very recently. Keep abreast of what's happening in the news, nationally and internationally. Don't ignore trivia – a good topical joke about a celebrity break-up or a fight breaking out on a sports field will really engage the right audience – and consider major themes that are relevant to your topic and the world at large.

There are also some personal topics that will always be relevant and have a universal appeal. Often these are centred around relationships, but remember to be careful to gauge the age and lifestyle of your audience before you launch into your anecdote; stories about children always go down well, especially if you have an endearing toddler story or a frustrating teenager one. Most of us can think of a time when our parents drove us mad, so that might be appropriate too. Work-based topics could fit the bill, especially if the experience is a common one, like too many meetings, poor communication or e-mail overload.

ACTIVE RESEARCH AND STATISTICAL INFORMATION

There is a raft of information you can gather that will contribute towards excellent future presentations. Do a self-audit, where you consider the type of subjects you are most often asked to talk about, then set aside time to find out some interesting facts. Statistics are good and carry great weight, but only if they are simple to digest; a long list of figures will only serve to baffle an audience and an overloaded slide, full of data, will do the same.

Try to stick to everyday issues – things that people can relate to. An example is the way that presenters often represent the size of something, relating it to 'equivalent to the area of four football pitches'. Where possible, try to find your own unique way of describing things, rather than relying on what has gone before. A senior marketing manager, responsible for encouraging tourism in Wales, once complained that the country was often used by news agencies to describe the area of something topical. Typically this had negative associations, for example: 'The ruptured tank has now produced an oil slick the size of Wales.' You can see his point.

Quirky 'facts' are equally good, and yes, the quotation marks do imply that the truth may have been bent a little. I am not advocating out-and-out lying, but by the way you present something your audience will often be forgiving if you use the adage 'never let the facts get in the way of a good story'. An example might be: 'Today, there is more computing power in a singing birthday card than there was in the entire world in 1958.' Even the most pedantic audience member is unlikely to take you to task over whether this is true or not. The point is, you're making a point! How much less interesting it would be if you painstakingly pulled together an estimate of the real amount of computing power, both then and now and, if the truth be told, your figures are not any more likely to be accurate than the original quotation. If you use the original quotation, your audience will quickly engage with the fact that you are illustrating how quickly, dynamically and massively technology has moved on, in a short space of time.

INDIVIDUALITY

If you buy in to the idea that an audience wants to hear you speak because you are unique, you can start to amass a file of material that reflects your own interests and personality. Developing an eye for what might be useful in future is about combining your past experience with the knowledge of what you aspire to present upon, some way down the line. News clippings, cartoons, facts and figures can all be amassed and kept in your own 'presenter's box file'.

Good idea

Keep a high level of awareness of all you 'consume' – stupid things our politicians have said on a news channel or a snippet of conversation overheard at a railway station are equally valid. With the material in the public domain, we can often go and look it up again later. All the best gaffes appear on YouTube, or similar sites at some time or another. However, with the overheard snippet of conversation, jotting down the relevant comment and filing it away for future use will pay great dividends, not least because it is likely to be unique to you and a reflection of how your personality sees the world.

Apart from the obvious benefit of having your 'presentation preparation muscles' exercised, you will be surprised at how useful your box file is in the future, when you sit down with a blank sheet of paper to write a new presentation. Often a piece of information that you have squirrelled away in the past will help to illustrate a point you want to make; occasionally, you might pick up a gem that is so good it can form the central core of everything you want to say.

The materials you collect are up to you. They need to have a personal resonance, otherwise you will lack conviction when you are presenting them. It is certainly true that building a file like this helps you with future presentations; it is a great way of 'unsticking' you if you cannot find anything to write. Remember when using any of this type of material to observe the principles of copyright law and seek permission from the instigator in advance and/or credit the original source.

USING QUOTATIONS

Quotations are a marvellous way of illustrating a point in a presentation, but only if they are chosen carefully, delivered skilfully and timed to coincide with the point you are trying to make. Strip the quote bare, uncover its real meaning and only then can you decide if it fits with your own content. An irrelevant quotation is worse than not using one at all. How you deliver a quotation is just as important; if you slip it in seamlessly, people will be more impressed than if you make a big thing of it.

It is worth emphasizing the need to consider the members of your audience and how important it is to connect with them. For example, bear in mind that displaying the literary prowess you gathered during your privileged education might just risk alienating one or two people. The following is an example of how not to do it: 'Wasn't it the great 17th-century French philosopher René Descartes who once said "Everything is self-evident"? And, d'you know, I think he was right.'

This is just pompous twaddle, especially pretending that you are trying to recall exactly who said this, when clearly you know all along. I have only used it as an illustration because I have sat in an audience when it was delivered.

As far as sources of quotations are concerned, life could not be easier. It used to be that you had to be tremendously well read to be able to deliver an insightful bit of wisdom from the classics of literature, now you just use a search engine. Ironically, when you are looking for a killer quote that fits the bill for today's presentation, you inevitably uncover all sorts of gems that are just not appropriate right now. Make sure you save them in your 'favourites', or set up a separate text document that you can index, according to subject.

Be careful with length and complexity. The best examples to use are the ones that are easy to grasp: the one-liners. If your chosen quotation is longer than that, it had better be making a substantial point and one that your audience will be able to follow.

Activity

Over the next week, make a conscious effort to start your presenter's box file by seeking out some relevant content that you can begin to collect. Newspapers and specialist magazines are always a good starting point, but if you need to extend your search further, try to gather some gems from the internet. Set yourself a target of a minimum of five quotations and three interesting articles.

SUMMARY

* Don't even begin to write until you have considered who the members of the audience will be. Find out as much as you can about them, right at the start.

* Tailor some content to the specific audience, but also keep generic material in mind that you can use across a variety of speeches.

* Stay alert to all the different things you can put in future presentations: illustrative stories with a good moral at the end, quotations, one-liners and jokes.

* When you come across great quotations, make sure you write them down or note where they came from so you can find them later.

* Bookmark good sources of material on the internet and keep separate 'favourites' folders by topic heading.

IT'S TIME TO WRITE... NOW!

So far we have looked at how to collect ideas together and at some of the factors that will influence your writing. I don't think we can put off the business of putting pen to paper any longer. This chapter begins by looking at how closely scripted you want your presentation to be and what medium you will use when presenting, then it moves on to look at five steps to writing a presentation.

Thinking about all the things you could say is rather different from sitting down and writing the presentation. Before you can begin, you need to decide on the level of scripting versus spontaneity. This will depend on a number of factors, including the length of the address you are going to give, how well you know the subject matter, and the level of formality of the event; for example, you wouldn't expect the finance director of a major corporation to get up, unscripted at the AGM. Here are a few different approaches to writing.

THE BIG SCRIPT

For the novice or the very nervous, the only form that the presenter is likely to feel comfortable with is the word-for-word script. If you are just starting out on the speaker circuit and are worried about forgetting something vitally important, this kind of scripting has its place. The upside is that you can stop worrying about what you are going to say, it is all there in front of you. The corresponding downside is that it is very hard to make this kind of presentation flow in a natural way.

I once saw a best man's speech at a wedding delivered like this and it was clearly important for the speaker to make sure he did not omit any vital element. There was the all important toast to make, a couple of embarrassing stories about the groom and a big finish with heartfelt good wishes to the happy couple. Clearly the pressure of doing a good job on such a big day was enough to convince him that a fully scripted address was necessary and, not surprisingly, his audience was happy to forgive him for this. In a business setting members of the audience might not be so sympathetic, they may want to see a bit more spontaneity.

WRITE IT, LEARN IT

For a really important presentation you might decide that you want to talk without holding a script or referring to notes of any kind. In this case you have no alternative but to write the speech long hand, learn it word for word and deliver it. It is tough and there is no shortcut, plus the fact that without cues you risk forgetting something or losing your thread, but the truth is that it looks fantastic if you can pull it off.

NOTES AND NUDGES

Somewhere between the two previous scenarios lies the middle ground occupied by a variety of notes, nudges and cues: the signals that connect the narrative together. This is where most presentations lie, giving a good balance of security (because you don't have to remember the whole presentation) and an 'easy', flowing speech (as long as you have rehearsed properly).

Two really good pieces of 'hardware' for helping to deliver this are cue cards and PowerPoint. It is better, in the early stages, if you don't try to use them together, otherwise you can get confused as to where you are. In the process of writing and rehearsing your presentation there is a funnel effect. When you first get started and are mapping out the content in detail, the cuing device (cards or PowerPoint slides) will contain a lot of information, so that you can follow the flow. However, as you hone down your story, you will be able to weed out any unnecessary words and phrases, relying only on the next memory jogger to move things on.

Cue cards

The great advantage of using cue cards instead of an A4 script is that you don't have it flapping about in front of you, distracting your audience and causing you stress as you wonder if you have the pages in the right order. As it is less obtrusive, there is a greater likelihood of your speech looking spontaneous. I have known professional presenters who use their cue cards more as a 'comfort blanket' than a script – something to refer to in case of emergency, such as total memory loss.

> **TIP**
>
> Use cards of around 12 cm × 8 cm, normally the kind you would have in a card index system. These are about the smallest you can get, but they will fit in a pocket until you are ready to deliver your speech, and if kept in the palm of your hand, the audience will hardly notice they are there.

How you lay out the card is up to you, but the example shown might prompt your own thinking. You will notice that the card is numbered in the middle and I always use both sides, to reduce the total number of cards I am carrying. I make it a rule to flip the cards over top to bottom, so the notes on the reverse side are upside down until you flip the card (unlike a book, the pages of which you turn side to side). It doesn't really matter which way you choose to do this, just be consistent, so that once you are in the swing of using cards they will always be formatted in the same way.

A hole punched in the top corner means that you can attach the cards together with a treasury tag to keep them in order, but for short presentations with only a few cards this is not really necessary. If, however, you do use this method, it can be handy if you have to make any last-minute adjustments to the order of your speech, as the cards can then be reassembled in a different sequence and fixed once more with the tag.

WRITING WITH POWERPOINT

The significant difference between using PowerPoint and cards is that when using PowerPoint you will be sharing the cues with your audience as you go along.

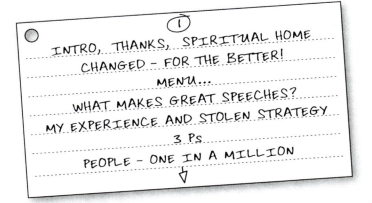

Figure 4.1 An example cue card

Most experts will tell you not to put too much information on your slides and you should certainly never reveal the whole story on them, otherwise the audience wouldn't need you there to explain it. You might chose to write bullet points that are a little bit cryptic, but don't make them so weird that your audience cannot see the connection between the bullet point and what you are saying.

The great thing about PowerPoint is that you can use its full breadth to help compile your story. When you become very skilled at presenting, you might deliver a presentation based solely on images rather than words, with each slide's image reminding you of the next point you wish to make.

Good idea

Try compiling a presentation where each slide contains just a single word. This is not only an interesting exercise, but also good practice for keeping the content of your slides brief.

Once you have decided which of the above methods you are going to use, you can begin the process of writing. One final aspect to consider before you begin is to think about structure.

- First, tell them what you are going to tell them. This sets up the presentation and manages the audience's expectations. It also 'trails' what's coming up.

- Tell them (present the ideas that you have just outlined).

- Finish by telling them what you have told them (reviewing and summarizing the central message that you have put across).

Working to this formula will ensure that your presentation has a logical beginning, middle and end. This kind of signposting also keeps audiences engaged and is part of any good presentation.

Activity

Watch any 30-minute news bulletin. It will follow a similar formula, opening with the headlines, followed by more detail on each story in order. Around 12 minutes into the bulletin the newscaster will pause to sum up the main stories and signpost a 'coming up...' section. Before the bulletin ends, a similar review of top stories will round things off. This is a great discipline for a half-hour presentation.

Coming up is a five-step approach to writing a presentation. To illustrate the process, I have set the task of writing a short presentation entitled 'What makes great speeches?'

THE FIVE STEPS TO GOOD WRITING

The big idea

Don't be intimidated by the blank sheet of paper, or screen, in front of you and wonder how you are going to fill your time slot. Once you get going, it is the editing down that is often the problem.

Start with a 'big idea'. Sometimes this is given to you as the subject of your speech; on other occasions, you will be expected to come up with it yourself.

The 'big idea' for the speech in this example is to focus on the fact that it is people who make great speeches. I know this sounds self-evident at this stage, but what I intend to show is that the uniqueness of the experience of a riveting presentation is down to the individual who is delivering it.

Three main points

The 'list of three' rule has really gained credence over recent years. I am not sure why, but I do know that it works. Limiting yourself to three points allows you to focus your mind on a small number of issues, not least because it makes them easier to remember and it introduces a level of discipline where you have to be ruthless in your editing of content. I am convinced it is much easier for the audience to go away with three key points, rather than a list of, say, 12. It also helps guarantee that everyone gets the same message as they only have a very few things to remember.

Let's look at the three main points I have chosen for this speech:

- preparation;

- practice;

- people.

The use of alliteration is deliberate. It might sound a bit of a cliché, but the truth is that when the points are spoken aloud, one after another, it gives a memory hook for the audience. It also gives you a better chance of recall later on.

Brainstorming the main points

Now that I have decided on the important areas I am going to cover, I need to be thinking of the sub-points I wish to make about each. To do this, I normally take a sheet of blank paper and write down all the ideas that come to mind, around that topic. Below is the kind of list I would generate for each of my three Ps.

Preparation

* Good speeches are the product of a lot of hard work in advance.

* An audience deserves to be treated with respect, so you need to prepare.

* There are many elements to a speech; they all need to be considered.

* Once the speech is written you will want to see where it will be delivered:
  - Room ergonomics are important.
  - Technical equipment is vital.

* Timing and length of the address need to be considered.

Practice

* Even professionals need to rehearse.

* Sounding confident is all about knowing your script.

* Listening back to a speech allows you the opportunity to edit and hone it.

* Less will go wrong if you have practised properly.

- You only have one chance for the live performance, practice will perfect it.

- The more rehearsed you are, the more relaxed you will be.

- Being relaxed will help you deal with the unexpected.

People

- Human interaction is what makes us remember great speeches.

- How the members of the audience 'feel' about the content depends on their reaction to the speaker.

- Part of all good speeches is persuasion. Only people can do that.

- Great speakers really engage with their audience.

- Each of us is unique; so, by association, is every speech.

- The person who delivers a great presentation will have prepared and practised (see above).

Developing the headings

Using these brainstormed ideas, the next stage is to think about what you will say on each sub-point. It doesn't matter too much if there are some bullet points that are more substantial than others, the weaker ones will be dropped in the editing stage.

Sometimes the acid test of these points is whether or not you can develop them at all. If you cannot, you might let them stand or drop them altogether. The stories you develop around each point might be from your own experience. It could be knowledge that you have uncovered through research, or you may have heard a story, or related evidence, that will help to bring the point to life.

Once you have 'bulked' out each point, you should have the majority of your speech written, but at the moment it is only a series of items on a menu. The next part of the process involves weaving these things together, so they make sense.

What's the story?

A television producer friend of mine once kindly agreed to review an idea I had come up with for a new television format. She listened patiently to my outline for a new lifestyle show, incorporating the magic television ingredients of cookery, parenting and happiness, and when I had finished said, 'Yes... but where's the journey?' That stuck with me.

In a presentation we are taking the members of our audience on a journey. At the end, they will have travelled a distance with us, but how will we have changed them? What will the narrative be?

If you are dealing with content that is fairly matter of fact, it is hard to weave this into a story, but in some ways that is all the more vital, if you are to bring it to life. This is important in keeping the audience's attention, but it is also a great way of helping you learn your speech. If there is some logical flow, if one element naturally follows another in the tale, you are much more likely to be able to commit it to memory.

With the example we are using here, you could personalize the content and 'attach' it to a character, for example saying this is how Trudy developed her presentation skills. You might even say what you have learned along the way, taking care to be self-effacing enough to recognize that the journey has only just started.

So, overall, it will help if your presentation is delivered in some kind of narrative style. However, this doesn't negate the need for stories within the broader picture. Storytelling, as part of your writing, is important enough to devote a separate chapter to, so it is coming up in Chapter 5.

The five-step plan outlined above for speech writing is a guide to get you started. This is because, for many of us, just putting the initial ideas down is the hardest part. If you discover a process that suits you better, that's fine too – anything that unblocks your writing.

I sometimes think a good analogy for writing is sculpture. You start with something that is vaguely the shape of the final piece, then mould it and refine it until it is ready to be presented to an audience.

Activity

Write something! Exercising your writing muscles is good practice for when you will have to compile a real presentation. Think of a topic you feel strongly about and sketch out the notes for a short presentation on it. If you struggle to think of a suitable topic, find out today's news headlines and develop a short speech that would outline what's happening in one of the stories. Take about half an hour on this, then if you are inspired repeat the exercise using a different topic.

SUMMARY

- Before you sit down to write, decide how you intend to deliver your address as this will influence how you approach the task.

- Get some ideas down on paper. Procrastination is the enemy of the writer.

- Use a staged process that has a logical flow. Either follow the five-step plan in this chapter or find something else that works for you.

- Lists of three work well when you are speaking. This can also help to make the writing stage easier, as it limits the number of ideas you will work on.

- Try to sustain a narrative through your writing as this will help the presentation flow and remind you of what comes next.

THE POWER OF STORYTELLING

In days of old, before pen and paper had been invented, let alone computers, people told one another stories. Despite all the technology we have developed since, the medium is as relevant today as it has always been and never more so than in making speeches and presentations.

Before we were able to write these things down, it was important to be able to pass on the learning of one generation to the next and so this was done by telling true, or illustrative, stories. Often there was a moral to the tale and this was there for a reason. With no formal law and order, there needed to be some code of values by which society lived, so stories always made some kind of a point at the end.

If we examine many of the fairy tales that are still told today, the key learning from them is as important as ever. However, there is another good reason why we pass on the learning in this particular format and that is because it is memorable; the learning is embedded in the narrative.

These two essential constructs of good stories, moral and memorability, make them an ideal vehicle for putting your points across in a presentation, where the audience may have nothing to take away at the end other than the experience of having listened to you. I can bear witness to the power of storytelling, as I can still recall anecdotes that I heard presenters tell 20 or more years ago – which is some feat, as I often cannot remember my own PIN number.

THE BENEFITS OF STORYTELLING

Storytelling offers these benefits in the context of a presentation:

- It helps you to illustrate your point. Some content can be dull and audiences might not engage with it very well, but a good story, well-chosen and delivered, can bring the issue to life and capture fresh interest.

- You can make a long-term impact with storytelling; the very fact that people might be able to recall what you told them in story form, much later on, shows that your presentation has the ability to affect behaviours or attitudes far into the future.

- A story adds to your popularity. It makes life easier for the members of your audience, so they will be much more prepared to listen to your whole presentation.

- Stories can make you seem more human. Really good presenters often have a clutch of stories that they tell 'against' themselves. Showing our own frailty says to an audience that we are all fallible; we are all in this together.

- A story brings light and shade. When the content you are delivering is heavy going, it is great to be able to lighten the mood and tenet of the speech with a good story.

- Stories provide you with anchors. Make sure the stories you choose are relevant to the rest of your content and you will have much less trouble remembering your speech. You might simply recall the stories, but then build upon them – you will have a ready-made outline.

- Storytelling can add to your confidence. Having some tried and trusted elements of presentation to fall back on is a great confidence booster; for example, I have a good 'technology' story that is a real banker if the PowerPoint ever fails. The added benefit is that while I spin it out, there is just a chance that a technical expert will get me up and running again!

So, stories have many benefits when we are presenting, but where do they come from and how do we collect them?

TRUE OR FALSE?

The first and most important thing to say is that stories don't have to be true, but don't abuse the privilege of the presenter by treating this lightly. Think about the professional comic who comes on stage and opens with the line 'A funny thing happened to me on the way here tonight...' We are all in on the joke, we know it didn't really happen; the comic is just employing a well-used set-up. So it is with many presenters' stories. They contain true parts, but we, the audience, are expected to suspend our disbelief for a moment, while the point is made.

Clearly you should never go to the extreme of telling a serious story that is completely fictitious and claim it to be the truth. To say that you were the CEO of a major corporation or once saved a man from drowning is only legitimate if true; otherwise, if you get found out, you will never be invited to present again.

Hopping along the line that is a continuum of truth, telling a story with elements of veracity, but much embellished, is fine. Often, for comic effect, you can exaggerate the level of the problem you were facing; for example, 'They asked me to set up the technical equipment, clearly not realizing that I'm the kind of guy who doesn't know how to switch on his mobile phone.'

COLLECTING STORIES

Good idea

Other speakers whose live presentations you have seen, or who you have watched recordings of, can be a good source of stories. Search online for these stories. Books and journals often contain excellent anecdotes and trade magazine articles are useful too. If you work in a specialist area, such as customer service or HR, subscribe to the relevant publications for detailed information about your profession.

Stay interested in other people too. Ask open questions about their background and how they got to where they are.

Even eavesdropping on a bus can yield a great story – just ask my mum!

There is a whole raft of sources for good stories and even if the stories are not particularly apposite when you hear or read them, you know better than anybody the kind of speeches you are asked to deliver, so can start to build up a file of stories for the future.

Of course, with any of these sources, it helps to know what you are looking for. Here is a quick list of a few business topics that might one day be relevant to your speech. As you meander through life, capture any stories you come across that might be handy later on.

Hot business issues

- Technology – collect stories on the pace of change, our inability to use technology, how powerful technology has become, how the cost has fallen, what future benefits technology might bring, think about how it looked when you were growing up.

- Economy – use stories that consider the state of the nation's finances; how you budget in your household; the fact that the more you have, the more you spend; whether we're in boom or bust – how you can tell.

- Conflict – issues for these stories include being made redundant, sacking people, boardroom battles, arguments in meetings, people who say 'with the greatest respect' when it is the last thing they mean, the stress of handling difficult situations.

- Compliance – areas for stories might be the burden of 'health and safety' legislation, the hoops we have to jump through, corporate social responsibility – why it is right to do the right thing, the pitfalls of non-compliance, changes in legislation.

- Communications – look out for stories about the burden of e-mail, using technology on the move, how ambiguity creeps in, communication breakdowns, the benefits and downsides of social networking.

- Achievement – material for stories might be what it is like to win, hitting targets and how that feels, setting goals and living them, what success means to you, planning the future, handling disappointment.

If your speech has a more personal agenda, with a different focus, draw up your own list of topics that you might cover in future, and actively track those stories down.

HOW TO TELL A STORY

There is quite an art to telling a story well and if you are going to make it work for you, then delivery is all important. We have probably all come across people who say 'I'm no good at telling jokes' and the same disciplines apply to both telling jokes and stories, which is worth noting if you intend to use humour as part of your presentations.

Top tips for improving delivery

- Know the story. This sounds obvious doesn't it? However, we have all been in a social situation where a husband and wife have interrupted each other during the telling of a story as one of them was 'getting it wrong'. Stories have a narrative thread running through them and to make sense you have to follow the sequence in order, otherwise you will lose your audience.

- Stick to the 'facts'. Whether fact or fiction, the important lesson is to tell what is relevant and leave all the other stuff to one side. Some people meander through a story with one digression after another, so that by the time you get to the end, you are simply dazed and confused.

- Paint a picture. Your words are usually all you have when telling stories, so fill in the kind of detail that will give your listeners a real sense of what was happening. If you were telling a tale of attending a lavish wedding, you might say things like 'champagne on tap', 'massive marquee' or 'palatial surroundings', just to bring the tale to life. Note this point in tandem with the last and be careful not to over-elaborate.

- Develop the characters. Good stories often entail great characters, so give a sense of who these people are. Again, the picture-painting technique of the previous point will come in handy. Include characteristics that are pertinent, so a sporting story would contain physical attributes, with phrases such as 'a huge guy' or 'fast as a greyhound'. A 'human' story might focus on more emotional elements, including comments such as 'so kind-hearted' or 'generous and thoughtful'.

- Use 'timing'. The pace and verbal delivery of a story can really add to its value. Think about the difference between telling a ghost story to a child or recounting the tale of a sales pitch to a work colleague. Tone of voice, speed, variation and sense of drama will change according to circumstances. Don't be afraid during a presentation to add some dramatic touches to your delivery. With practice, they will enhance a good story even further.

- Go beyond – apart from the basic constructs of the story itself, what is it saying? There may be an obvious moral at the end, but if not, be prepared to spell it out. In a presentational context, you need to be able to relate your story directly to the content you are delivering.

- Practise. You see, I could not get through the whole of this chapter without mentioning this, yet again! If you are thinking of using a story in a presentation, look for opportunities to give it a few 'dry runs' to see if it works. In a smaller gathering, perhaps socially in the bar after work, see if you can slip the story into the conversation and gauge the reaction. This will start to indicate whether it will work on a bigger stage.

Activity

Write three stories about things that have happened to you, using just 50 words to summarize each. The topics are as follows: 'That's when I knew it had all gone wrong', 'Oh, the benefits of youth!' and 'My hero'. How could you embellish each or any of these to make a point about who you are?

SUMMARY

- Storytelling is an age-old way of embedding learning; people remember good stories for ever.

- A well-chosen anecdote can add weight to your argument, both on a logical level and in an emotional sense.

- Practise turning your observations of human nature into stories, as these are the kind that resonate most with a variety of audiences.

- Compile a mental list of topics and start collecting stories about them. They will provide a springboard to your writing in the future.

- Use every opportunity to have a go at storytelling. The improvement in your technique will amaze you.

USING HUMOUR

Being funny can be the best way of making a terrific presentation. I say 'can be' because humour is like dynamite – fantastic if it explodes in a spectacular display of fireworks, less good if it goes off in your face. This chapter follows on from those on writing and storytelling as the subjects are interrelated. It can be that humour is truly spontaneous, a reaction to something that happens on the day, but more of that later; for now, some guidance on how to amuse your audience.

APPROPRIATENESS

The first rule of humour is to question whether it is appropriate. All the things we have so far considered about audiences, the type of presentation you have been asked to give, the prevailing mood at the time and the circumstances of the speech are important.

I think there are very few occasions where some form of humour cannot help to put your message across. Just because you are delivering 'dry' content about the company's annual accounts, for example, doesn't mean you cannot throw in the odd one-liner, if only to check that the audience is still awake. In business, it is often the case that people can find amusement in the darker side of an issue. Here is a great example.

Humour in times of adversity

The term 'gallows humour' conveys the idea of humour in times of adversity particularly aptly! This type of humour can be found in most situations, often expressed by the very people who are facing adversity.

When the former telecoms giant WorldCom hit the buffers, its staff kept their sense of humour. After weeks of plummeting share price, amid rumour and gossip, the NASDAQ suspended trading on 26 June 2002, when the share price fell to 9 cents. Internally in WorldCom, the accounting scandal came as a shock to many. They had been unaware of what was happening, but as is often the case in these circumstances a cloud of gallows humour hung over the offices. When a rallying memo was circulated saying 'Our customers can count on WorldCom to meet their communications needs, today and tomorrow,' someone added to the bottom 'Friday is sort of doubtful.'

When it comes to good taste, stay well on the 'safe' side of the line. If there is any chance you might offend with a remark, then don't say it. Racist, sexist, ageist or overtly 'cruel' material are no-go areas, with the exception of when the comment is gentle and self-deprecating. For example, a man talking about his inability to multi-task, when compared with female colleagues, goes some way to balance the normal prejudices that women in the workplace face. A more mature speaker can rage against the baffling march of technology in the same way.

The other side of the appropriateness coin is that there may be some circumstances where humour is not only appropriate, but virtually essential. If you are trying to enthuse an audience and have been asked to deliver a 'rallying cry', it will be much better received if you are able to do it with a bit of wit thrown in. Equally, if an audience is being expected to listen to a full day of platform speakers and the rest of them haven't raised a titter, it is all the more important that you are able to lift the mood a bit.

ARE YOU FUNNY?

Appropriateness is one very important criterion to use when thinking about whether or not to attempt humour. Another one is your chance of success.

All of us are funny in our own way. We all have times when we make others laugh, but controlling this and delivering it, to order, is another thing entirely. In the movie 'White Christmas' actor Danny Kaye delivers the line (when talking about himself) 'I know this guy, he's kinda funny in living rooms...', which helps to sum up the contextual nature of humour.

There is an acid test that applies to humour – and it's pretty hard to argue with. Do members of the audience laugh? If they don't, you are not funny, so bear this in mind the next time you think you have a killer line or hilarious story.

Like all of the gifts we might be born with, good looks, intelligence, sporting ability (but enough of me), humour is just one more. Some people are just 'naturally funny'. What is encouraging for the rest of us is that practice can help to perfect whatever level of 'funniness' we have inherited.

Even top comics have to work hard to get their humour to be funny. One of the current crop of British funny men recently admitted to spending six hours a day working on his material and yet when he (or his peers) crack a one-liner, we think they have just thought of it.

PLANNED VERSUS OFF THE CUFF

I love the expression 'a well-rehearsed ad-lib'. For me it sums up the nature of comedy – that when it is done well, it really does appear to have been made up there and then. As just outlined, virtually all good comedy is meticulously planned.

If you witness a really good business presenter doing the same address twice, you might be surprised at how much of the content, which appeared spontaneous first time around, is actually incorporated in the second address.

The more planning you do, the better your real ad-libbing becomes. This is mainly driven by having the confidence to attempt a punchline that has just occurred to you, safe in the knowledge that if it doesn't work that well, you still have your practised material to fall back on.

No one can tell you how to be funny off the cuff. If it comes to you, it comes to you; if not, you cannot force it. Having said all that, if you keep your eyes open to the absurd, if you are prepared to use self-deprecating humour – which I would recommend – then there are often situations when you will simply spot a comedy element in what is happening around you.

WHAT TO EXPECT WHEN YOU DELIVER A FUNNY LINE

In professional comedy circles there is a technique called 'riding the gag'. Comics have been doing this since the days of Max Miller and Jack Benny and it is still as prevalent today. Essentially, it means that you should never look as if you are expecting a laugh. Instead, you just carry on regardless and only pause if the amount of noise makes your next line inaudible. This changes the dynamic between you and the audience from one of 'Look at me, aren't I funny?'(which happens if you deliver the punchline, stop and wait for the audience to laugh) to one of 'Gosh, what a surprise, you found that funny.'

You can see this in action for yourself if you look out for it the next time a comic appears on television. Contrast this technique with Jim Henson's Muppet creation Fozzie Bear, a supposed comic, who would deliver a line and await his laughter. Poor Fozzie usually 'died' on stage at the hands of aged theatre-goers and professional hecklers, Stadler and Waldorf. This is to be avoided if possible.

JOKES VERSUS ANECDOTES

A good joke, delivered well, at an appropriate part of a presentation, in keeping with the rest of the content and in tune with the kind of audience before you is a fantastic way to endear yourself. But – and you've guessed it, it's a big 'but' – there are lots of risks associated with jokes.

First, it is usually pretty obvious that you are purposely telling a gag, making it much harder to 'ride it', as we saw above. By contrast, if you tell a story, especially one against yourself with an ending that (you hope) will amuse, you can keep on going, only stopping if the audience breaks out in spontaneous mirth.

WHAT TO DO WHEN HUMOUR FAILS

The next thing about jokes is that they are not all funny and what makes one person or group laugh might leave another cold. If this happens, the resulting silence is an awful thing to contend with, but you just have to carry on regardless. Don't draw attention to the lack of laughter, just keep going and hope that when viewed as a whole, no one will remember your one moment of embarrassment during the presentation.

Jokes 'do the rounds', so you forever run the risk that the audience have heard a joke before. In most cases, the nature of a joke that leads to a punchline (which, technically speaking, works because it is unexpected) means that it is never as funny second time around.

Even funny jokes are not worth telling during a presentation unless you can relate them to the rest of the content. The members of the audience may enjoy the light-hearted intervention, but will end up asking themselves what point you were trying to make.

Finally, jokes have a kind of context. In a club, late at night, when people are relaxing with friends and may even have had a drink or two, they are ready to laugh. First thing in the morning, at a conference, with a hangover, they may be less so. Be warned!

THE ART OF EXAGGERATION

The wackier and more exaggerated a story, the greater the likelihood of getting a laugh, so you might begin with the bare bones of a real story, but blow certain aspects up to make them ridiculous. Often, people in an audience can spot themselves in this and presenting a larger-than-life version is a great comedic ploy. For example, being an obsessive list maker is a more common trait than you might expect. When you start talking about how you have a master list of all your other lists, it is funny. As the old journalistic adage goes, 'Why let the truth get in the way of a good story?'

TOPICALITY

A topical story is not necessarily funnier than other stories, but it does have the added benefit of showing that you are 'on the ball' – that you know what's happening in the world and are quick-witted enough to be able to make some kind of humorous reference to it.

> ## TIP
>
> It is worth thinking about the 'world' that the audience is living in. Some of the knowledge will be the common ground, which we all share, such as news and current affairs stories, but it will probably extend beyond to celebrity gossip, knowledge of sporting events or the plot of the current soap operas. Apart from what's happening on a world stage, take your topicality down to a local level too. Find out what people in your audience are thinking about. If presenting within an organization, find out, for example: is the company undergoing expansion? Have those in the audience just won a major piece of business? Are they relocating to plush new offices? Whatever is on their day-to-day agenda is fodder for topical humour.

In conclusion, there simply is no better way of getting the members of an audience on your side than through the use of humour. They will warm to you, listen more attentively to the rest of your presentation and, as a consequence, remember a greater amount of what you say.

For this reason, I would urge any speakers to use their natural humour as much as they can. Don't force it, feed it in gently, a bit at a time, until you are confident with it, and whatever you do, never look as if you were expecting a laugh. When it comes though, you can accept it gracefully.

Activity

Think of something you are sometimes criticized for. This is the starting point for a story that is self-deprecating. Is it your sense of direction, inability to master technology or obsessive tidiness? Now consider an extreme situation, tailored to whatever the trait is. What was it that drove other people mad about it? How did it resolve itself? What did you learn? Where possible, try to make the witty anecdote something other people would relate to; either as the 'perpetrator' (appealing to all the obsessively tidy people in the audience, for example) or the 'victim' (which will resonate with all those who live with a tidy person).

SUMMARY

- Funny is good! The most popular presenters are the ones who make their audiences laugh; it is the best way of engaging.

- As always, think about the audience. Don't even consider delivering a story or joke until you have worked out who will be hearing it.

- Ride the gag. Don't look as if you are waiting for a laugh, if it doesn't come, just keep going.

- Begin with stories; they are safer. If you master this art and are brave enough, move on to telling jokes, but make them relevant.

- Look for topical humour on the day of the presentation. What's in the news that morning? What is preoccupying the minds of the people in your audience?

WHAT'S THE POINT OF POWERPOINT?

As you are reading this, someone, somewhere, will be working on a new presentation tool they think will revolutionize the industry. Maybe they are right; but before we get too fixated on what is available, or what might come on the market soon, I think it is worth taking a step back to consider what role these add-ons play.

Visual aids have been a part of presentations for decades from the primitive days of the humble flipchart through to the overhead projector, with its accompanying acetates, to 'electronic projection' via computers using (mainly) PowerPoint and on to multimedia displays on whiteboard technology. Why do we use visual aids though? Not many presenters stop to consider this question, as you will know if you have ever watched someone read out every word on a PowerPoint slide before flipping to the next one and doing the same, ad nauseam.

However, if used well, visual aids can do three things. First, they can form the structure of a presentation, which is especially useful for you when you are faced with putting it together; slides tend to lead us to big ideas and so ordering those in a way that is logical will help in forming your core. Second, when you are on your feet in front of the audience, these visual aids can act as a prompt to what you are going to say, replacing a full script or even cue cards. If constructed well, the visual presentation will lead you to tell your story in a logical and well-ordered way, without necessarily giving all the information. The third benefit of good visual aids is that they should enhance your monologue, adding some new information, presenting ideas in a graphical way that makes them easier to understand, or providing a visual stimulus, such as a dramatic picture that will complement your words.

These are the basics of visual aids and some presenters wouldn't even think of getting up before an audience without them. On the other hand, there are really powerful speakers who never use them; I cannot recall an iconic speech from history that used PowerPoint. Becoming a really professional presenter might mean being able to operate in either set of circumstances.

For now, let's take it as read that there will be plenty of times when you will opt to use a tool like PowerPoint. What do we need to do to get the best out of it? Chapter 8 will have a similar round up of tips for you when using other visual aids.

POWERPOINT BASICS

The frightening thing about PowerPoint is its power! Like lots of technological products it has a multiplicity of features built in that most of us will never use, but maybe that is not such a bad thing. For the sake of argument, I am assuming that you have at least a basic working knowledge of the tool; if not, there are many ways of getting up to speed, from courses at your local college, through to step-by-step tutorials in the package itself.

If I had my way, I would put a ban on people learning to use the fancier features of the program, but I dare say Microsoft would feel differently about that. The reason is that many presenters get fixated by the 'bells and whistles', forgetting that the content is the important thing and even this pales into insignificance alongside the power of the presenter – yes, that's you.

The way slides animate is a pet hate of mine. I simply think it detracts from what you are trying to say, so I would never use a checkerboard wipe or fly the letters on one by one. What does it add?

DEVELOPING A POWERPOINT PRESENTATION

Start at the beginning, with the structure of your presentation before you, and decide a rough running order of slides. You don't need one to explain every point, just the major ones and the junctions between sections of your presentation.

In terms of slide design, uniformity is the most important thing. Changing any element of design from one slide to another looks sloppy and unprofessional, so either use the template your organization has designated, or choose a simple one from the menu in the package.

Good idea

Where possible try to avoid strong or dark colours as a background. Not only can they make slides difficult to read if you choose the wrong text colour, but they can also make them a nightmare to print, if you decide that your audience may want a copy to follow along with.

Stay with plain black lettering or a neutral shade; dark blue works well for text. Pastels tend to get 'washed out' against a light background and this can be made worse if projected onto a screen in a room that has a lot of light in.

Font (the style of text) and point size (the size of text) should follow the same rules of plain, simple legibility. Where possible, try not to have variations of text size from one slide to another. How large your text is will really depend on how much of it you intend to try and fit on each slide, but remember what was said earlier about 'less is more'. If you have already set the size you want to use, be aware that the program will reduce this automatically if you try to fit too much onto any one slide.

You have maybe witnessed presentations where the speaker flashes up a slide and says 'I'm not sure if you can read all of this...' or 'There's probably too much information on this slide...' which is really unforgivable. If the presenter knows this to be the case, why on earth has this slide made the final cut and become part of the presentation? The worst example I have seen was the head of communications of a large organization, who continually apologized for the befuddled nature of her slides; that's really ironic.

Good PowerPoint technique

A picture can represent 'a thousand words', so using graphics often brings a point home much more succinctly than text alone. My own preferred layout is opposite (Figure 7.1), showing a main title, three or four bullet points down the left-hand side and an image or graphic that helps to emphasize the central message. Keeping your bullet points short is a good discipline to get into. It means they will act as a prompt for you to be able to expand on; it keeps your slides uncluttered and necessitates your being there to explain them, rather than the scenario I outlined earlier, where you could give the audience the presentation and not bother turning up.

If you think back to Chapter 4, on writing, part of the technique was to strip the presentation down into basic ideas and then develop each of them. You can build a story in this way, via a succession of slides, each of which adds to the previous one. It is better to have more slides with less content than to try and cover everything in one go.

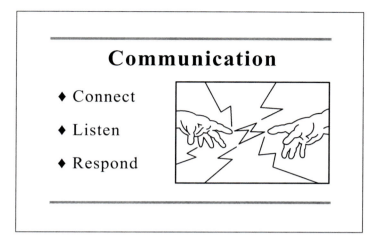

Figure 7.1 A simple PowerPoint layout

If you have a concept that requires you to present, say, eight bullet points, then I would suggest splitting it across two or even three slides. However, if you find yourself having to use more than this, it is likely that you are trying to present something too complex. Look instead at the component parts of your presentation and decide if you can strip it down further, to simplify it.

TIP

Another good technique for maintaining interest is the 'question and resolve': the first statement you show is in the form of a query, to get your audience thinking, the same slide then shows the answer. It might be that you enhance the quiz element of this by offering A, B, or C multiple choice answers to stimulate thinking before you show the solution.

PowerPoint gizmos

Common add-ons to PowerPoint presentations include the use of remote controls and pointers. A remote control allows you to roam the stage, flicking to the next slide at will, but if because of nerves you get a little 'trigger happy' you may find you have skipped a slide and want to go back. Most remote controls have this facility built in, but it might result in you getting a bit flustered, especially if it happens at the beginning of your presentation before the nerves have really settled.

There are simpler alternatives; you can simply return to the lectern and use the key on your laptop to change slide, or if you are in a well-supported facility, there may be an operator at the back of the room who is changing the slides for you. Either arrange in advance a 'cuing' system, where you will nod to the operator when you want the next slide, or simply cue in verbally, by saying something like 'On the next slide, we'll see...' Make sure your operator is well briefed in advance and wherever possible have a run through with the operator before the audience arrives.

Pointers direct a beam of light onto the screen, so you can highlight a bit of your slide from a distance using the red dot that is projected from the pointer. As with all technology, if you use this well you can enhance the look of your presentation, but overuse will annoy the audience. It may be that you can do without a pointer if your slides are well constructed in the first place; instead of using a pointer you may simply say, 'The second bullet point here, which describes the "silo mentality" of the organization, is the important one...'

There are whole books dedicated entirely to the use of Power-Point and it is, without doubt, a great presentation tool. I believe that if you take a plain and simple approach to using it, you will never go far wrong.

Activity

Play with PowerPoint! Take just 20 minutes to navigate around the PowerPoint screen, checking out the drop-down menus and searching through the options. You will probably find all kinds of hidden surprises. If a feature appeals to you, make a few dummy slides using it and save this as a template for use when you have a real presentation to deliver. If you have the time, search online under 'PowerPoint tips'.

SUMMARY

- PowerPoint is a tool to enhance your presentation, not replace you. Make sure it adds to what you are saying in a complementary way.

- Slides can act as your prompt, so that you don't need separate notes or a script, which will free you up to be a better presenter.

- Simplicity is the key. You don't want your audience to be distracted by some of the fancier features of the program.

- Be consistent in everything you do. Slides should have a standardized format: keep colours and text the same across the whole presentation.

- PowerPoint is a visual aid, so use images and graphics to add something to your words and keep the audience's interest.

OTHER VISUAL AIDS

There is nothing wrong with relying on PowerPoint to help you write and deliver a presentation. I am a big advocate of this. However, if you are going to be truly professional, you need to be able to look beyond the norm and develop skills across a range of different visual aids.

This will not only broaden your skill base, but will also allow you to choose the right tool for the right speech. In a room of 12 delegates a flipchart will normally suffice, but with a bigger audience you might need something slicker. Trying your hand at different presentation methods should also include, at some point, delivering without the help of any of these tools – just you, your words, your voice and your passion.

AUTOCUE OR TELE-PROMPT

The technology of the television newsroom has migrated to many presentation facilities over recent years, so at some point you may be called upon to present from an autocue-type machine. If you have never seen these close up, they are simply a device for projecting a script, so that you can read your speech while appearing to look at the audience. In television news, the autocue is positioned directly below the camera lens, giving the impression that the newsreader is looking straight at the viewer.

Live presentation versions have monitors placed flat on the floor below you, with perspex 'screens' mounted on stands in front of your eye line. There are normally two screens positioned at 'ten to' and 'ten past', if you were to think of the 'o'clock' as being straight out in front (see Figure 8.1).

As you read the script from the perspex screen, the words scroll upwards, so there is always a 'feed' of your next line. Some systems are self-operated, so you can speed the text up or slow it down; however, I wouldn't recommend them unless you are very skilled,

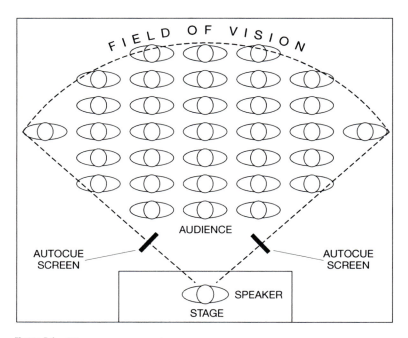

Figure 8.1 How autocue works

completely relaxed about your presentation and fully in command of the technology – and I have yet to meet that person.

A much better way of mastering the art of autocue is with the help of an operator, who has a copy of your script and your best interests at heart! The text normally rolls at an even pace and can be set faster or slower, but we don't read evenly. Instead we pause at the end of sentences and sometimes, for dramatic effect, our speech alters in pace, depending on what we are saying. All of these variations need to be taken into account by the autocue operator. It is harder than it sounds.

Mastering the technical side of autocue is a matter of practice – the more you do it, the better you will get. However, this type of presenting relies more heavily on pre-preparation than any other, in the respect that the script you produce is critical to your success.

Writing a presentation word for word that sounds 'natural' and conversational is a real art. If you want to know how natural your script is, the very least you must do is read it aloud. Even better is to record it and listen back with a critical ear. Try to notice the words that you would not usually use in an everyday chat or the phrases that sound as if they are part of an official document, rather than something someone would naturally say. If possible, get a second opinion from someone who you trust and go through the script line by line.

Now you might think that this next bit sounds obvious, but believe me when I say that I have personal experience of training really senior people in use of autocue who had not spotted the following flaw in their plan. When you 'load' your script into the autocue program, you have quite a bit of leeway for what I would call 'technical editing', so you can reformat the text to make it larger or smaller and add breaks.

The size of text needs to be just large enough for you to be able to read comfortably, but no larger. If you sometimes wear glasses, quite obviously you will need to change the text size to suit. The bigger the text, the less of it will fit on the autocue screen at a time, so don't overdo the text size or you will end up with the thing whizzing along at a right old pace. Avoid big sections of text. They are hard to read in a natural way and if you glance away from the screen for a second you will then struggle to find the point in the paragraph where you paused.

Put your breaks in at the points where you would pause during normal speech and don't worry about this giving a fragmented appearance to the script; it's about being able to read it easily. The final addition to your presentation is optional, according to how complex it is and how confident you feel about the autocue, but often professional speakers will add 'stage directions' to the script, in bold and in brackets (so that they don't read them out by mistake). This will include instructions such as (pause) and (play video insert). With practice and the help of a good operator, you can even up the level of spontaneity by breaking off from the script at a prearranged point with a stage direction such as (tell redundancy story).

To use autocue as it is intended, you need to be able to read alternately from one screen then the other, so that changing your eye line will make it look as if you are scanning members of the audience, looking at them. When you are really skilled you can read from one side, look to the front and deliver the next line (which you have just seen on the screen), then pick up from the tablet on the other side. Really, it's not as complicated as it sounds, it just needs, you guessed it, practice.

Generally speaking, autocue does not easily allow for spont-aneity, which is one of the killer applications of a great present-ation. The ability to go off script (at least for a moment) to comment on something that has just become relevant, such as the sun coming out, a crash of dropped plates from the adjacent hotel kitchen or someone laughing loudly at one of your jokes, is a much undervalued tool of professional presenters. There is also little room for ad-libbing, perhaps to make a joke about something that has just occurred to you. For these reasons I find autocue a little restrictive. Each time you decide to go 'off script' you do two things. First, you give your autocue operator a heart attack – the operator will have to stop the machine dead and cannot be sure when you will pick up the prearranged script again. Second, you put more pressure on yourself to find where you were on the screen before your witty interlude. If you 'fumble' this, it is like dropping the baton in a relay race. You can never recover, because you will have admitted to your audience that you are reading a script rather than delivering an address. Yes, I know that they already know this, as audiences are media-savvy enough to understand what autocue is and what it does, but they will sort of forgive you if your presentation is seamless. Otherwise they will condemn you for not having learned your piece and then exacerbating the situation by not being able to read properly!

If you haven't got the message by now, then read my lips as I narrate from the autocue, 'This is a very difficult tool to use. If done well, speaking from autocue can be brilliant, but make sure your script is perfect before you start and rehearse with the technology until you are fully competent.'

There, that didn't sound too bad, did it?

FLIPCHART

At the other end of the technological scale is the humble flipchart. Use it for small, informal presentations, speeches or training sessions. Flipcharts are often overlooked in these high-tech times, but, if used well, I think they have still got a place in the presentation skills toolkit.

Perhaps where they score most highly over their jazzier counterparts is that there is not much that can go wrong with them.

If you have a collection of half a dozen flipchart sheets that you have prepared at home, rolled up and taken to the venue along with some reusable adhesive putty, I cannot think of anything that would stop you from being able to present when using them. There are no issues with power, availability of laptop and projector, or compatibility of formats; they are just ready to go, when you are. Here are some additional handy hints to get the best out of using flipcharts.

● You can prepare in three ways: prepare the flipchart sheets at home; in advance of the presentation, ask that a blank flipchart pad is provided, then get to your venue early and prepare the sheets before the delegates arrive; or draw them 'live' in front of your audience.

● Keep the content simple, as you would with PowerPoint. A few bullet points will be enough, or a big drawing to represent a point. Don't plan to write lots of text as this takes time and you will lose the audience's attention.

● When you are writing on a flipchart, try to stand to the side of the easel and reach your arm across, so the audience is not presented with your back and can see the words as you write them.

● If you 'brainstorm' an idea with an audience, it is OK to end up with an overloaded, cluttered flipchart sheet. It shows how many fantastic ideas have been generated. As the presenter you will then have to make some sense of it.

● If you have prepared flipchart sheets in advance, mark them up with a sticky note attached to the edge, like a tab, so you can go straight to the one you want, instead of flicking back and forth with a look of panic on your face because you cannot find what you are looking for.

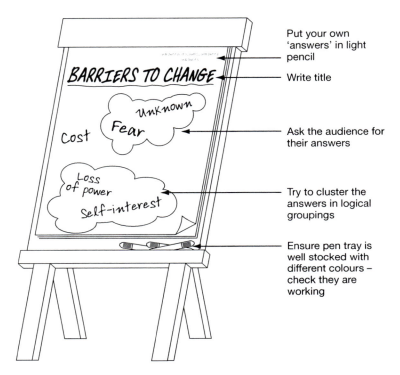

Put your own 'answers' in light pencil

Write title

Ask the audience for their answers

Try to cluster the answers in logical groupings

Ensure pen tray is well stocked with different colours – check they are working

Figure 8.2 Using a flipchart

TIP

If you are going to call for answers to a particular question, write the answers you have already thought of in faint pencil at the top of the flipchart page. Your audience won't be able to see this list from a distance and it makes you look as if you have great knowledge, and a much better memory than you really possess.

ELECTRONIC WHITEBOARD

In professional 'classroom' environments, the tool of choice is now the electronic whiteboard, sometimes also known as a smartboard, which offers the opportunity to combine multimedia elements for a really polished presentation.

Although a whiteboard is still largely an academic tool, it is not hard to see how the prominence of this method will increase as more and more facilities install whiteboards. Any of the applications you currently use on a laptop can be employed on a whiteboard, with the added bonus of being able to write, highlight, erase and move elements around the board, as you would by clicking and dragging with a mouse. The icons on whiteboards follow a similar pattern to that found on standard computers and because many of the features are the same the navigation round the board is very intuitive.

Sounds, text, video, graphics, games and quizzes are all fairly standard features that are great for presentations where interaction is a key feature. New developments are coming on stream all the time, as manufacturers compete to become the first choice in this technology.

If all this sounds a little advanced from where you are now, cast your mind back 10 years to the kind of computer technology we were using then. This should be a great comfort to you, because we all tend to adapt to the new features that are offered to us, as we go along. Common sense dictates you wouldn't even think of 'going live' with a whiteboard until you were very much in command of the technology: training is required.

Activity

Find out more about the visual aids you are less familiar with. If possible, have a go at using autocue or a whiteboard. The latter shouldn't be too difficult if you know any teachers, for example. If you cannot get hands-on experience yet, check how the experts use this kind of technology, by searching online resources.

SUMMARY

● If you have a choice of visual aids, select the one that best matches the job in hand, taking account of audience size and the objectives of your speech.

● Say 'yes' to autocue only if you have plenty of time to rehearse in the actual facility with the operator who will be there on the day.

● If scripting for autocue, seek out a second opinion from someone who will tell you if your words sound natural.

● Don't forget that the simplicity of flipcharts mean that they will never let you down. Their only restriction is their limited size, so small audiences are needed.

● The future will inevitably be whiteboard or a derivative. Begin thinking about which multimedia elements you could bring to your presentations.

REHEARSAL

I am not saying that the writing part is easy, but great presentations are really made in the rehearsal phase. By the same token, the converse applies if you don't prepare enough. You can never expect to be a polished performer – it's that simple. Time then to move on and look at how you take your well-crafted words from the flatness of the printed page and, through trial and error, breathe life into them, as a finished presentation.

A famous golfer – there is some dispute about which one – once said 'The more I practise, the luckier I get.' It's as true for public speaking as it is for golf.

But how, when, where and what amount of rehearsal is needed? This chapter is here to guide you and answer these questions.

Back in Chapter 2 we looked at keeping a 'sense of proportion' by asking: What is this presentation for? Who is it going to be delivered to? What is riding on it? When you have answered those questions you can start to form a mind's-eye picture of you performing. Will you be wandering the stage, unfettered by notes or slides, passionately delivering a seamless speech you have learned word for word? Or is it sufficient, under the circumstances, to stand behind a lectern with a script in front of you and a carefully worked-out PowerPoint presentation?

Keeping things in perspective and deciding on your delivery method will drive all your ongoing rehearsals, because they will determine how you wish to appear to your audience. Here are some options:

* You might seem fully learned and brilliantly spontaneous.

* You might make occasional reference to notes or slides.

* You might rely heavily on scripted content.

Depending on the length of your address, it is possible to mix and match some of the elements above to produce a really excellent finished speech. If you have learned five minutes of impassioned content as a slam-bang opening and are able to kick off with this, you can then turn to some form of notes and your audience will happily forgive you. Make sure you link the two sections, so you don't look as if you have just lost your thread. Finish the rallying cry with 'So, that's what's before us, these are the challenges we face and if you think it looks tough, it is. Let's take a few minutes to examine what we can do together to make this next year a success.' Then move to the lectern, to continue, with PowerPoint or your written notes.

When it comes to rehearsal, the mistake lots of rookie presenters make is they have the general outline of their speech, so they think it will just all come good on the day. It may be they have structured this with PowerPoint, have written copious notes or have jotted some bullet points on a sheet of A4 – not good enough!

REHEARSAL TECHNIQUE

Out loud

The only way to know if your presentation is going to hang together, when you deliver it out loud, is to deliver it... out loud. Not muttered under your breath, but standing up and spoken, in circumstances as near to how the real thing will be as possible.

I am often to be found strutting round my office, spouting forth on some topic or other, as a precursor to a 'live performance'. The curious thing about doing this is I find it often influences the content in a quite dramatic way. Once you start to hear back what you have written, it is surprising how many times you think 'No, that just doesn't work.' Any really well-honed presentation will be as a result of a process like this.

If your speech contains a joke (be careful – see Chapter 6) or some storytelling, this is a reminder you really need to become so familiar with it that it flows in a seamless way. If either of these are badly delivered – for example: 'Oh no! Hang on, was it the manager who said "Don't you know who I am?"'... Or was it the CEO?' – you will be much worse off than if you had not bothered telling the joke or story at all.

TIP

You might choose to rehearse out loud, in front of a trusted colleague or family member, so you can get some feedback. This is often more nerve-racking than standing up in a room full of strangers, but it is a good way to improve your performance.

Duration

There are two important things to say about the length of your speech. The first is it should be however long you have promised; the second is it should be paced. Let's look at each aspect separately.

Really slick, professional presenters don't go over their allocated time, nor do they come up short. There are a number of good reasons why they are able to do this. Through hard-won experience and practice, they may have an off-the-shelf presentation they have delivered many times before and so know it fits a particular time span. Alternatively, by having written and delivered presentations over a number of years, they have got used to interpreting the amount of written material they have into a time frame. It is like knowing that to present a typed script at your normal pace runs to around two and half minutes per sheet of A4 – that's just my pace, it's worth checking your own.

Pacing

If you are a little less experienced and are delivering a completely new presentation, then this concept of pacing is critical. It is done by developing a modular presentation, with primary and secondary messages, that can be 'flexed' as you go along. This means having a core set of points with supplementary content, for example a selection of illustrative stories, that can lengthen the speech if you are coming up short or be dropped altogether if time is running out.

A word of warning

Be careful not to have too many slides in your presentation if you need to be flexible with your delivery. There is nothing worse than being 20 minutes into a half-hour presentation knowing that you have only covered 5 per cent of your slides. Audiences get a bit restless if you say, 'We'll skip the next dozen slides', as they wonder what they are missing and you look ill-prepared.

Modular presentations work best with fewer slides that can be 'talked up' or briefly described, according to how your timings are going; then only you will know what you have skipped or lengthened.

You may think that it seems like quite an advanced technique to rewrite the script in your head as you go – and it is. However, it becomes easier, surprisingly quickly, when you deliver lots of presentations.

The really clever bit is to do it without members of the audience noticing (see the box 'A word of warning', above). You don't want them to feel short-changed by not getting everything you have prepared or to think you such an amateur that you have got the timings badly wrong.

A good trick is to have a presentation with a number of 'break points' in it as this will give you the breathing space to make adjustments to the length of your spoken content. This might be as simple as showing a video clip. Then while the audience are watching, you can check where you are up to, assess how much content you have left and make some instant editing decisions if necessary. Alternatively, you might set the audience a simple task, like thinking of three things that inspirational leaders do. While they are busy, you can do a bit of rejigging.

The final important thing to say about pacing is that you have to consider your entire piece in terms of the pace it is delivered. It is fine to add a bit of drama by having a slam-bang opening or a rousing finish delivered at a punchier pace than the rest of the talk, but, overall, you need to aim to keep it even. Suddenly rushing through the last six slides will alert your audience to the fact that you have messed up the timing and are trying to shoehorn too much into a short time frame.

Time it

It makes sense that you will only know how long your presentation is if you time it. Most mobile phones have a stopwatch function now, so use this to get an accurate picture of how long you are speaking for. If you stop to make notes or amend your presentation while you are rehearsing, don't forget to pause the clock too.

When it comes to 'real life', you will find many presentation suites have a clock at the back of the room, so the speaker can check the time. If not, take your wristwatch off before you start and prop it up on the lectern, so that you can keep track of the time without the audience knowing. Part of professionalism is about doing what you have promised to do and that includes speaking for the exact duration you have been given.

Recital

How well should you know your presentation? The answer is based on a number of factors. To help you decide, consider the following:

* How long is the total speech?

* How often will you have to deliver it?

* How do you want to be perceived?

* What are the expectations of the audience?

* How easily do you memorize?

The older we get, the harder it is to commit things to memory, so be more selective about what you choose to put in your speech. That said, if you are going to deliver the same speech time and again, make the effort to memorize as much of it as possible.

Later, we'll look in detail at the importance of the start and end of your presentations, but for now I would like to emphasize that it is worth the effort to try and get these sections 'off pat', especially the opening, as this will help to settle your nerves.

Stories and anecdotes are also quite easy to remember (which is why we use them on our audiences), or if you have constructed a presentation around three key points, you should be able to recall them easily enough. However, if you want to learn to remember material more easily, are there any helpful ways of going about it?

MEMORY TIPS

- Turn the entire presentation into a story in your head. If there is narrative flow, you will remember what's coming next much more easily. When you are at the writing stage, make sure the sequence of steps is logical, leading towards a moral at the end.

- Use alliteration on your main points. For example, you could talk about the 'three Rs' as personal attributes of managers: resilience, resourcefulness and reflection. The points are much easier to remember in that format.

- Divide up your script and learn it in bite-size pieces. Try to master one section completely before moving on to the next. As already mentioned, learn the start and end sections before anything else.

- Record and play back. Commit your speech to a recorded format. Most mobile phones have this facility. When you listen back in the car, on your commuter journey or when cooking dinner, try to anticipate the next bit before it arrives.

- Stand and deliver. When you have a reasonable working knowledge of the presentation, try a dummy run, making quick mental notes of the bits you struggled over. Pretend it is a real-life scenario and go from start to finish as best you can, before reviewing the sections you know less well.

On the subject of rehearsal, let's close by posing a question. Can you rehearse too much?

I don't really think you can. The better you know your material, the more scope there is to put some real meaning into it. If it is a constant struggle to recall the next thing you are going to say, you haven't got much brain capacity left for thinking about how well you are delivering.

Striding around the office, or at home reciting your latest speech might make you feel daft (and scare other people), but compare this to how stupid you could end up looking if you forget during a presentation what you were going to say. If that doesn't make you uncomfortable enough to take rehearsal seriously, nothing will.

Activity

Write and memorize a three-sentence generic opening to a speech. This could include something about the venue (regardless of where it is), a few words about yourself and/or the reasons why you are delighted to be making this presentation. Make sure you can deliver this opening without hesitation.

SUMMARY

● Begin by deciding how much of the presentation you are going to commit to memory. This will drive your rehearsal schedule.

● At the very least, learn your opening and closing lines, so you have a strong start and finish.

● There is no replacement for rehearsing out loud; only then can you get a real sense of how you will sound on the day.

● Concentrate on keeping an even pace throughout the speech and reflect afterwards on how well this worked. What could you do better next time?

● Use the memory tips in this chapter or find your own ways of learning material off pat.

FINDING YOUR VOICE

So far, the brief has been set (either by someone else or to your own agenda), you have written the content, added some interesting stories and rehearsed until you feel ready to hit the stage. Next we come to the actual delivery of your speech, a key part of which is the sound of your voice.

We hear our voice partly through our ears but also by the sound waves travelling through our skull, owing to a thing called bone conductivity. This is why when we listen to a recording of ourselves speak, it comes as a shock and the more we protest to those around us that it doesn't sound anything like our voice, the more they assure us it does. So, the best thing is to get used to it.

In extreme cases, people have set about changing their voice radically. One such example was British Prime Minister Margaret Thatcher, who in the 1970s was coached by a television producer to lower the tone of her strident voice by 46 hertz, to give depth and authority to her speech. If you too are thinking of running for office, then please feel free to take the same route; otherwise, stick with what you have got, with a few minor tweaks (see below).

Regional accents are fine, as long as they are not so broad that anyone from outside your town would struggle to understand you. How much of our natural accent comes through can vary according to circumstances. For example, it may become thicker when you are at home and almost disappear elsewhere. My voice gets a little 'posher' when I am presenting – though these days, not much, I've pretty much got used to the way it is – and hits its zenith of sophistication when I am recording my voicemail message or answering the telephone.

And it's not just me, I have noticed this in friends and colleagues too, so I can only surmise lots of us do it, which must mean it's OK! I am simply cautioning against trying to alter your natural state too much, because you think it will make you sound better to the audience. If you put on a voice and are not very good at it, you will just look (and sound) foolish. So, whatever your inclination for adapting your sound to your surroundings, go with that and no more. Leaving aside our 'natural' sound for a moment, there are lots of ways we can work on our voices that will make a big difference to the power of our performance.

VOLUME

You might well say that if, in these days of technology, you are increasingly going to be amplified by a microphone when making a presentation, it doesn't matter how loudly, or quietly you speak; the equipment will be set to compensate for this. However, there is what I would call a minimum level, a point where a voice becomes so quiet and 'weak' that the audience will begin to doubt your conviction. If you are going to look confident, you have to speak out, strong and proud. This is something you should practise during your rehearsal phase.

I don't want to scare you too much by harping on about my personal presentation disasters, but there have been a few occasions when the microphone has failed. I have had to rely on being able to speak out sufficiently loudly to be heard at the back of the room.

Rise and fall

Sound engineers everywhere are going to hate me now. During the course of your address, according to what you are saying, your voice should rise and fall – in volume not pitch (as you don't want to sound like a swanee whistle) – to exaggerate the points you are making. Go online and watch some of the classic speech makers of our day and you will soon witness them doing this. As with all these techniques, try it out a bit at a time until you gain a mastery of it, otherwise you might risk it sounding false.

A great speech will benefit through this rise and fall. It adds interest, draws the audience in and builds credibility in what you are saying.

PASSION

Show some emotion. You can do this through your voice. The rise and fall we have just examined will happen much more naturally if there are parts of your presentation you feel really strongly about. Pause a moment and think about the difference in your delivery if you were presenting the company's annual results, as opposed to speaking on behalf of a charitable foundation seeking to alleviate starvation and suffering. Now, inside your head, try to hear the difference in your voice. That is the difference the audience will witness if you can get really fired up about parts of your address. This is something that is almost impossible to fake, which is why audiences love it so much.

PACE

Slow down! That is the general rule for the infrequent speech maker. It does require some degree of concentration, as there is a physiological reason we go too fast, especially at the start. Our natural 'fight or flight' response has been triggered and we have gallons of adrenalin pumping through our system – no wonder we go at it like an express train.

Again, as your confidence grows, you get used to controlling the pace of your speech and once you have mastered it, you can think about how to tie it together, in conjunction with the 'rise and fall' discussed earlier, to add further interest to the overall sound of what you are saying.

UMMS AND ERRS

I have no idea why it is, but it seems to be getting harder to avoid the tons of 'verbal garbage' that chokes what we are trying to say in an articulate way. I have to try really hard to eliminate the 'umms' and the 'errs' – and when it comes to the 'y'knows', even more concentration is required. Only about one in 50 people have the ability to speak naturally without all this wasteful punctuation. When you really think about it, you can do it, but it does, y'know, take effort.

It is worth finishing this chapter by looking at the work of Albert Mehrabian from the University of California, back in the 1960s. The Mehrabian study (Figure 10.1) looked at a range of factors that might influence an audience's ability to become engaged and interested in a speaker. Over half (55 per cent) of the impact of a performance came from non-verbal factors, such as confidence, appearance, demeanour and posture, so think hard about these when you are reading the relevant sections in this book. Of the rest of the factors, 38 per cent fell into a category

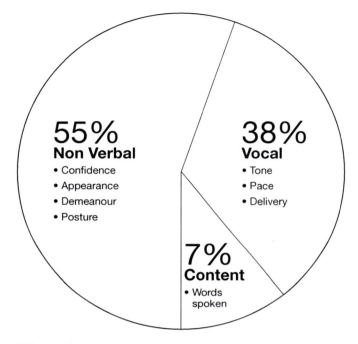

Figure 10.1 Mehrabian study

that could broadly be called 'vocal' – tone, pace, etc (see above). You may have worked this out – that leaves only 7 per cent of influence from the actual words spoken. So this is important stuff, but don't lose focus, you still have to deliver the words!

Although the results of the Mehrabian study might look extreme, evidence to support them can be seen in the political arena where prior to elections presidential or prime ministerial debates are televised. Often the winners of these contests are judged more on their performance than by what they said.

Activity

Record your voice in a variety of circumstances and settings and listen back to it. You might always be conscious of when the recording is happening, but try to ignore this and just be yourself. Balance up the more informal, social situations with some more focused business scenarios, including when you are presenting. Go beyond the first response of not liking the sound of your voice and try to review the recordings objectively, so you can improve your vocal projection.

SUMMARY

* Use your own voice. Don't try to copy or mimic another accent or the delivery of a different speaker. Make the best of who you are.

* Be prepared to speak out, loud and clear. A microphone will carry your voice to the back of the room, but you also need to display confidence in your tone.

* Avoid the pitfalls of pace. Make a conscious effort to slow down in order to articulate your words properly.

* Stay conscious about the sound of your voice and what you are saying, so that you can try and vocalize seamlessly.

OPENINGS

Although the importance of opening your speech strongly has already been mentioned, we haven't yet covered the best way of doing this. This chapter looks at the 'hows' and 'whys' of openings.

Good idea

Before you think about stepping up to the podium there is a prior stage of preparation, which is to think about how you would like to be introduced. What your host says to welcome you to the stage will begin to influence the audience, so if you want to stay in control of this, you will need to write your own introduction, keeping it short – and witty, if possible – or brief the person who is introducing you on what to say. This will make life much easier as you start your speech.

From a structural point of view, the opening of your presentation is, without doubt, the most important part. The reason the first few sentences you say are so critical is that they have a huge influence on everyone in the room: members of the audience and, just as importantly, you the presenter.

From the point of view of those in the audience, how you start is who you are; they will make their minds up very quickly. As you want the rest of this performance to go well, it is critical that you get them on your side, right at the top. Although engaging people is really important, making sure you don't disengage them in the first few minutes is even more important. Lots of speakers do this, simply by not having a strong, positive enough opening.

TIP

Never, never, never

Never begin a presentation with an apology. Whatever might have gone wrong, you need to open with a positive comment, before acknowledging the broken air conditioning, the failure of the PowerPoint or the lack of natural daylight. The only thing a speaker should have to apologize for is being late, but that never happens to professionals like you.

FALSE STARTS

In many presentation situations there is a minefield of 'false starts' to be navigated. Distractions can get in the way of launching off in a positive way. Some of these are foisted upon us by others, such as where the organizer asks if you will announce where the toilets are and the fact that no fire alarm is expected today. This kind of 'statutory requirement' may be unavoidable, for the sake of health, safety and comfort, but avoid making it the first thing you say. Get your 'big opening' out of the way first, then backtrack to this sort of dull information.

Surprisingly, many of the false starts you hear are nothing to do with the organizers, but down solely to the haplessness of the presenters themselves. How many times have you heard an opening like these.

'Hello, can you hear me at the back?'

'There are still a few more stragglers to come, but I think we'll get started.'

'Did everyone get a pack with the slides in it when they arrived?'

These are not openings, they are disasters. Professional presenters don't get distracted by worrying whether their audience can hear them; they have already sound checked the room in advance. The same applies to the other examples; they are just audio wallpaper, contributing nothing useful and getting in the way, spoiling what could otherwise have been a great opening.

These are all classed as 'false' starts, because members of the audience were expecting to hear a slam-bang introduction to whatever the presenter was going to talk about, not some trivia that doesn't affect them or that can be dealt with in another way.

Don't let distractions derail your opening. This is most likely to happen because of latecomers, but remember that it is their fault they are late, not yours. You have no obligation to make them feel at ease for sneaking in after everyone else. In fact, if you do, you are sending out a signal that says 'Hey, it's OK to turn up late, it's only me you've come to listen to.'

My advice is that you ensure in advance that the entry door will not break your line of sight with the audience, so that latecomers are not forced to walk across you to get to a seat. Instead, make sure the room is configured so the stage is at the opposite end to the entrance.

The next thing you do is completely ignore the latecomers. This does two things. First, it says you are in control, and secondly, it marginalizes them, rather than glorifying their entrance. If you are running a full-day conference and you are the main speaker throughout the event, it is much less likely that people will return late from the breaks if you adopt this behaviour.

Most latecomers are already embarrassed by their inability to arrive on time and therefore effect the 'late walk'; a sort of tip-toed lilt, like you used to see in Tom and Jerry cartoons when the characters were trying to be quiet. There are a few latecomers who will huff and puff and apologize noisily, even offering some kind of excuse. The same applies, ignore them completely.

THE NEGATIVE START

False starts are bad, negative ones even worse. If you begin on the back foot, why on earth would your audience want to stay and listen? Again, examples to make you cringe are listed below and in case you think that I have made them up, I haven't: they are all real.

'Errrm... I'm not very good at this sort of thing...'

'This next section is a bit boring, but...'

'I'm not sure why they've asked me to speak...' – Hey there, if you're not sure, how the heck do you think we, as your audience, feel?

Audiences can find a dozen reasons to dislike you, based on your clothes, hairstyle, voice, demeanour, etc. Don't give them one more!

TOP TIPS FOR BRILLIANT BEGINNINGS

The kiss of death will befall your presentation if you start with a dull monotone voice, if your opening slide fails to capture the imagination of your audience or if you don't give them any good reason to listen to you – but enough of the negatives, how do you wow your audience from the word go?

Set the right tone

From the very second you stand up to speak, your audience will begin to make a snap judgement about what the next half hour is going to be like. Whatever you decide to say as your opening line, the really important part is to look like you are in control. There's nothing that unnerves an audience more than a presenter who looks unsure. The tone of your opening should do two things: it should say something about the kind of presenter you are: are you businesslike and matter of fact, which might be appropriate at a sales pitch? Or are you chilled out and witty, as an audience might expect from an after-dinner speaker? Next, it should signal the kind of content you are about to deliver. For example, a really good opening joke made at the start of a speech about cutbacks and redundancies might be regarded as inappropriate. Similarly, if you are speaking at a relaxed social gathering, beginning with statistics about the recession is a bit of a passion killer.

Agree or disagree

Whatever the topic, there will be some arguments in favour of the case and some against, so it is a good idea to have an opinion! It is unusual to be asked simply to outline a case, including the pros and cons, in order that the people in your audience can make up their own minds. Much more likely is the scenario when you are asked to speak up for something or refute it.

In the same way, if you are asked to cover a business topic, such as the benefits of using a 'balanced scorecard' to measure performance, your opening statement should say where you stand. Let's say the members of your audience are fans of the balanced scorecard. To grab attention you can tell them one of two things: either that everything they thought is right and that the balanced scorecard is the Holy Grail of measurement, bestowing upon its users untold riches and power; or that the whole concept is complete rubbish. The latter option is riskier, but I suppose you had already worked that one out. The greater the risk, the higher the potential reward, so your statement is likely to grab the audience's attention right from the start. You then need the confidence and sound arguments to back up what you have said.

Of course, you can fireproof yourself from controversy by blending both options. You begin with the controversial statement, go on to present your arguments and conclude that the principles of the balanced scorecard are valid – they simply need to be applied in the right way. By doing this you have grabbed attention at the top and reinforced the viewpoint of your audience by the end.

Make 'em laugh

Having a witty opening line is a great way of getting the audience on your side and, just as importantly, helping to relax those tensed-up nerves. There is a distinct difference here between a joke and a witty observation. I have cautioned against joke telling already in case it doesn't get a laugh. If that happens at this early stage in proceedings, it will increase your nervousness.

Witty observation is less risky and often funnier. The state of the economy, a big news story or the nature of your competitors can all be worked upon for a witty one-liner. The usual rules apply about taste and decency and you had better add appropriateness as well. Don't forget to take account of the members of the audience and their particular sensitivities.

A massive step up the scale of brilliant presenters can be taken if you are able to tailor your wit in a topical way. If a universal truth about the lunch you have all just eaten, or the room you are in or the journey to get to the venue occurs to you, then this will really impress your audience. Tread carefully, as ever. It's fine to make a cheeky comment about the catering, but if this spills over into out-and-out criticism, you need to remember that someone in the room will have been responsible for organizing it. Maybe it was the CEO who insisted on that particular menu... oops!

Tell it straight

There are some circumstances where it is better to leave the comedian back in the dressing room and present in a much more matter-of-fact way. If that is the case, you might decide it is best to 'cut to the chase' right away and simply tell it straight.

An example might be as follows: 'In the next 20 minutes, I'm going to do everything possible to convince you that choosing us will secure a long-term, credible, cost-effective supplier relationship that will help to underpin your own business success.' Sometimes, straight is good.

Be complimentary (but not fawning)

If you really are happy to be in Harpenden, or delighted to be in Denver, then it's fine to say so, but you need to be genuine in your sentiment, or the members of the audience will think you are just spinning them a line.

A bit of forethought or research might help you here. Showing you have taken the time to find out about the urban regeneration scheme for the city you are in, or the success of the local sports team, will carry some weight. What is better is if you have a personal anecdote of time spent in the place, for example: 'The last time I was here, my hosts were so hospitable I can't really remember much about the visit. That's why I've had to come back!'

If you can't find a connection, then a contrast can be just as good. Think about where you live, or were born or brought up. Can you reference this by talking about town versus city? Insular versus cosmopolitan? Even European versus US culture? Cultural differences can be a real source of interest. You might even have a story that illustrates this – I know I do!

However you choose to open, keep it snappy. You don't want to lose your way right at the top, or give your audience the impression you may have done so. This tends to rule out long anecdotes or descriptions.

Be absolutely cast-iron sure of the first words that are going to come out of your mouth. Don't rely on 'busking' it – don't ever think 'I'll start with something about the awful weather we've been having', like a stand-up comedian. Hit them with your first line, rehearsed and rehearsed and perfected, square between the eyes.

TIP

It's not all about me... me... me!

I used to feel so unbelievably flattered if I was asked to speak at an event that I thought it a good idea to justify my presence to the audience, as if I couldn't really believe it myself. On more than one occasion I started with a mini-resumé of my career and what made me suitable to stand before the audience. I think this was a big mistake, not because I now believe I am so brilliant that I need no introduction or justification, it's only that I should be able to prove my worth, my suitability to the event, through what I say and how I say it. Let's face it, if my presentation is rubbish, they won't care if I am Emeritus Professor of Public Speaking at Harvard – not that I'm sure this actually exists – they will still be bored.

The other thing that happens when you launch off on a long list of 'me, me, me' stories, is you come across as a bit of a big head. Humility is a much more endearing trait; it's better to be a bit humble.

Activity

Write an opening for the next speech you have to deliver or, if necessary, an imaginary one. Read it out loud and think about how it sounds from your point of view. Now, read it again and try to consider objectively what impression it would make on you if you were a member of the audience. This is a good way of testing your opening lines.

SUMMARY

- Avoid the negative. At the start, stay in control by making a positive statement that asserts who you are.

- Ignore any distractions, especially latecomers. Start on time and don't be put off if anyone enters the room after you have begun.

- Be relevant and appropriate. Think about the needs and wants of the people in your audience; the more topical you are, the easier it will be to engage them.

- Say something nice. Be complimentary to your hosts, or about the venue, town or city you are in.

- Rehearse your opening few lines, so you can deliver them unscripted and with confidence.

ENDINGS

For now, let's not worry about all that important content in the middle of your presentation. Let's just fast forward to the end and think about how to get off the stage.

In many ways, endings can be more difficult than openings, often because there is an element of uncertainty over what will happen next. Will you take questions? Is the audience expected to burst into spontaneous applause and mob the stage? This is what I usually expect; I can't think why I'm so often disappointed. Or will the host take to the stage to bring on the next speaker? There are so many variables that it is up to you to grip the thing by the throat and have it done your way. Let's begin by dealing with how you finish.

MAKE THE ENDING DEFINITE

Don't fizzle out into nothingness. After all the hard work you've put in, you deserve to have a slam-bang ending. I have heard speakers who have said:

'Well, that's about it really...'

'There's more stuff in the notes if you want to read up later...'

'I think I'm probably out of time, so I'd better stop...'

Your end sentence should be written and rehearsed just as rigorously as your opening. It should have impact, it should leave no doubt that you've finished, and it should end 'Thank you.'

MAKE IT UPBEAT

Maybe I am stating the obvious when I say finish on a high, but you would be amazed at the number of presentations that don't. In many cases, this is because speakers simply haven't thought of having an upbeat ending. They may round things off nicely with a comprehensive summary of what they have said and finish by thanking their audience for listening, but it is hardly inspiring stuff.

Optimism is the key here. Whatever you have presented, even if the content has been doom and gloom laden, you have to leave your audience believing things will be better tomorrow; there is a bright new horizon and the future is filled with exciting opportunities. Often, it is in the face of adversity that great orators emerge. I think this is related to their ability to make the audience believe things can only get better.

MAKE IT TIGHT

From a structural point of view, think about how the last five minutes of the presentation is going to go. The summary will be pretty familiar territory to you. Most of us summarize as a matter of course. You also need to clear the decks of 'parish notices' as they are sometimes called, for example what happens next?

When the coffee break will be? Is there going to be a question and answer session? You may even need to introduce the next speaker. All these 'domestic' issues might be important to the smooth running of the event, but they make rubbish endings to your presentation. Get them out of the way before your big finish.

Leave yourself a minute right at the end, to deliver your well-written, carefully rehearsed, tightly packaged finale. Build towards it and at the appropriate moment, stop. Your applause will follow.

A good lead in to these last few sentences might be as follows:

'I've talked about some serious issues today; we have, without doubt, some exceptionally difficult challenges to meet; but I'd ask you to remember one thing...'

Or alternatively:

'Out of everything I've said today, there is one thing that stands out for me as more important than anything, and that is...'

MAKE IT PASSIONATE

As we have outlined, passion – really caring about something – is one of the key ingredients great speakers harness.

It's fine to let your feelings shine through during the course of your presentation, but I would say it is essential to give them full rein as you reach the end. Speak from the heart and your audience are bound to warm to you as a person.

A footnote to all this is that 'passion' does not always entail shouting. Some speakers seem to think hectoring the members of the audience is the best way to convince them that they mean what they say, but passion can be quiet. It can be determined, it can be as much the look in your eye as the tone in your voice. If you really mean it, you don't need to worry about how this will come across, your natural feelings will carry you through.

ONCE YOU'RE DONE

The whole business of managing the audience's expectations is one of the essential tools of the accomplished presenter. People don't like ambiguity and it is especially important to bear this in mind when you come to the end of a presentation. They want to know what is going to happen next and you can govern that. For the sake of argument, let's say that you have agreed to run a question and answer session, between the end of your presentation and the run up to coffee break in 10 minutes' time. This is how the sequence of events will take place.

Outro

1 Manage expectations: 'This has been a complex issue and I'm happy to take some questions in our run up to coffee break at 11 o'clock, but before that I want to finish by reiterating one important point...'

2 Passionate ending – call to action, rallying cry, plea for support.

3 Bang! You shut up.

4 Applause (rapturous, obviously).

5 Question and answer session.

6 Round off the question and answer session with a final rallying cry.

7 Coffee.

APPLAUSE

I have attended hundreds of 'fizzle-out' presentations, where not even the merest ripple of applause has broken out at the end. Applause is important for a couple of reasons. First, you have worked hard to write, rehearse and deliver this presentation. You deserve some reward for it and an appreciative audience is usually enough payback for most of us.

Second, and this is the vital bit, applause makes the audience feel better. They are sharing with their fellow delegates in a positive feeling, brought about by what you have just told them. Why wouldn't they want to break out into spontaneous clapping?

TIP

Did I say 'spontaneous' just then? Well, if you do it right, delivering the ending according to the plan, then yes, it should result in people showing their appreciation.

However – and don't think worse of me for this – you can pretty much guarantee applause if you have a few 'clappers' planted in the audience. Naturally, people are reluctant to start a round of applause if they think that they might end up being the only one clapping, but they are all too ready to join in once the applause has kicked off. Make sure you have briefed your 'clappers' properly, so they know the cue. You don't want to be interrupted half way through because of their over-zealousness.

A quick final note about national culture. It is not too much of a stereotype to suggest that Brits are more reserved than their US or Australian counterparts. Remember that the territory you are in might have an effect on the readiness to applaud!

Activity

Complete the following phrase: 'My passion is...' Now, write a 100-word piece that would serve as an ending to a speech on this topic. Read it back, then edit it down to just 50 words. This should give you a powerful ending.

SUMMARY

- Never fizzle out! Make your ending purposeful and definite and leave your audience in no doubt you have finished.

- The last thing you say is the point the audience will remember the most. Choose the single, most important point from your presentation to finish on.

- A good, strong ending keeps the control with you. It will help to make you look assertive and confident.

- Audiences like to know what's going on. With a well-planned ending, you can manage their expectations.

- The applause resulting from a strong ending leaves a positive feeling in the room.

HANDLING YOUR NERVES

You will feel nervous, it is inevitable. Mark Twain once famously said that there are only two types of speakers in the world – 1: The nervous and 2: Liars. And he was right.

Sometimes, just the thought of having to speak in public is enough to increase your heart rate, so by the time your turn comes, it feels as if your heart is almost thumping out of your chest. Like all things though, with practice, you get less nervous and become better able to deal with it. I bet you cannot wait for that day!

However, for the time being, here are some calming words of advice on how to handle nervousness. Begin by attempting to rationalize your feelings. What exactly are you frightened of? Most of the time, it is simply a desire not to look stupid. If you are well prepared and have rehearsed properly, it is highly unlikely that you will look stupid.

Most of us also want to look professional when we are presenting and it can be hard to do this if your voice is wobbly and your hands shaking. All I can tell you is audiences rarely notice just

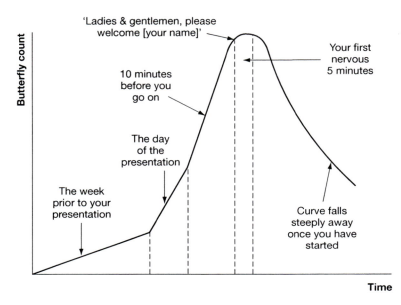

Figure 13.1   The nerves curve

how nervous a performer is – presenters are better at hiding it than you might think – and these physical symptoms rarely last more than a few minutes, at the start of a presentation.

I would go so far as to suggest there is a kind of 'nerves curve' presenters go through (see Figure 13.1). Our apprehension builds as the time for us to speak gets closer. It peaks at the point we begin, but starts to trail off after we have got through our opening remarks. This is one of the reasons I think it is so important to write and rehearse the start of your speech so thoroughly.

The antidote to nerves is confidence. The more you can do to bolster your confidence, the better. That means being prepared, not just for the way you plan things to go but also for a few contingencies. What is your plan B if the PowerPoint fails? Or the room is laid out all wrong? It is easy to see how being prepared, communicating your needs clearly, in advance, and knowing your presentation sufficiently well, you could deliver the 'bones' of it will all mitigate against these potential disasters.

ANTIDOTE TO NERVES – CHECKLIST

* Prepare – cover all the bases, including the contingency planning.

* Practise – make sure you have mastered your presentation before you arrive. You don't want to be rehearsing right up to the last minute.

* Stay in control – don't let other people's lack of preparation hijack your professionalism. Turn up, be gracious and do what you promised to do.

* Be early – even if you have to sit in the car park for half an hour. Better that than rushing in, hot and flustered, at the last minute.

* Avoid stimulants – don't drink caffeine for an hour before you present, otherwise you may find it will make your heart race. Never drink alcohol before a speech.

* Hydrate – sip water before you get up (to stop your mouth drying) and keep some handy, near the lectern. Be careful not to knock it over!

* Breathe – if you stop doing this, you won't be able to present, or do anything else. Take a deep breath before you start and don't rush.

* Concentrate – get the first few sentences out of the way, then let your nerves start to calm down all by themselves.

BODY LANGUAGE

In order to avoid looking nervous, many people put too much emphasis on controlling their body language in pressurized situations. I am not dismissive of the concept that how we are feeling inside is 'leaked' out to people around us, by the unconscious posture, actions and mannerisms we display; however, there is not a lot that we can do to address it at a conscious level.

Let me give you an example from real life. You may have been in a high-pressure situation in the past, such as a job interview, when you have suddenly become conscious of your body language. You are sitting there, with your legs so tightly crossed they have wound around each other like a jungle creeper. Your upper body is bunched and tense and your arms are folded tightly across your chest. You simply couldn't look less relaxed. Suddenly you remember all about body language and uncurl yourself, to sit in an open, pseudo-relaxed mode. Two minutes later, you have forgotten again and are back to being almost foetal.

The point is, if you are going to get your body language right, it is much better to deal with the *cause* than the symptoms.

Genuinely find ways of relaxing and your body will follow. Simply reminding yourself to alter what is your 'natural state' will only result in you reverting to it all too quickly.

By now you will have followed the earlier advice and learned the opening to your presentation. Visualize how you will look as you deliver it, rehearse it time and again, in front of the mirror if necessary, and let this well-practised 'opener' become your gateway to calming the early nerves. Footballers, ballet dancers and singers all get nervous before they go on, but once their performance is under way, the jitters soon disappear. Master this technique and let the body language take care of itself. After all, you've got enough to think about.

Before we move off this subject, it is worth saying a few words about our natural style. Some so-called experts will tell you to minimize your expansive arm-waving gestures or instruct you to stay still, for fear of distracting the audience, but I take the opposite view. I think it is much better to display your natural style, because it helps to express who you are. For example, it would be unthinkable to have a conversation with Italian people who didn't use their hands to express themselves and I have always found that their gestures added to what they were saying rather than detracted from it. The exception to this rule would be to check, by watching a video of yourself, that you don't have any truly disturbing nervous ticks; anything else is fair game.

And a final word, because we can get a bit twitchy and nervous when on stage we do have a tendency to fidget more than usual, so take any loose change or keys out of your pockets, so you don't start 'jangling'. Only carry in your hand what is necessary, such as your cue cards or script. This will save you the temptation to indulge in behaviour that will distract the audience.

Face up to the fact that being nervous is an emotional reaction. For most of us it will always be there and you can take heart that most professional speakers think it is a good thing. When you stop being nervous is when you start getting complacent.

Activity

Before your next presentation, make a disaster checklist. On a sheet of paper, write down everything that could feasibly go wrong that would prevent you from being your best. With each item on the list, consider what action you can take now to mitigate the risk.

SUMMARY

- Being nervous is natural. Don't be surprised or disturbed about it, every good speaker feels the same at some point.

- Confidence is the antidote to the jitters, so look for every available opportunity to build it.

- Prepare properly and you will minimize the risk of things going wrong, thereby reducing your worries.

- Let your body language take care of itself. Too much effort concentrating on this will mean you run the risk of making mistakes with other aspects of your presentation.

HANDLING YOUR AUDIENCE

We have established that the audience is probably the single, most important factor when considering a new presentation, but what exactly is 'an audience'? How can we get to know it better? How can we be more in tune with it and encourage it to respond positively to what we are saying?

We can much better understand the DNA of an audience by raising our consciousness the next time we are part of one. How do we collectively react? What is our individual role in that? The truth is that an audience goes beyond the obvious and predictable behaviours of a collection of individuals and gains a momentum of its own, based on overall group behaviour.

An example of this, which we touched on in Chapter 12, is the subject of applause. When you are in an audience and the applause starts, think about the point at which you join in. Usually there is a tipping point, just after the first few handclaps. It is as if most of us are waiting for our cue, eager, but afraid to start the process off.

This principle can apply across all audience behaviours. Laughter sparks laughter; booing encourages booing, as anyone who has ever experienced the uniquely British experience of Christmas pantomime will testify. (Let's hope there will be no booing when you are speaking.)

As well as being driven by the behaviour of the group, audiences are also affected by many other factors. Their mood can be determined by expectations, so it is very different trying to get a reaction from a 'cold crowd' first thing in the morning on day one of the conference compared with being the speaker after dinner on the final evening.

Watching comedy can tell you lots about audiences. Many professional comedians have a support act whose job it is to get the audience in the right mood. Television has used this trick for years, employing a professional warm-up act before the main presenter comes on. This tells us audiences gain momentum. Once an audience is in a good mood it is much easier to sustain the positive ambience.

FEAR OF THE AUDIENCE

I don't mean how afraid you are of the audience, but the other way around. Audiences are often nervous of us; anxious that we will meet their expectations, looking for clues that we will deliver, hoping that we will be engaging and will not overrun.

Nobody turns up to a performance, whether it is a conference address or a stand-up comedian's routine, in the hope that they will see someone 'die' on stage. An audience likes to be put at ease, right from the kick-off, by seeing confidence and competence, so that is what we need to deliver.

When it comes to openings, try to remember that the audience, in general, is a timid creature. It can be easily frightened, so don't kick off with anything too intimidating – unless it has a specific shock purpose. If you ask a question as an opener, make it a rhetorical one; don't expect an answer! Here is an example:

'Is it just me, or has technology just got too complicated these days...?'

Follow this up, quickly with something like:

'That's the question I was asking myself as I sat on hold, waiting for the IT helpdesk to respond.'

NEVER CRITICIZE

There are lots of reasons why the members of an audience can be tough. They may have been forced to come to the event, the three feet of snow outside might be a clue as to how bad their journey has been, the threat of redundancies in the organization may have dampened the mood a little, or the speaker may be hopeless. If the last reason applies, then tough, you just need to weather the storm.

You can try everything you know to get the members of an audience to like you, but in the end, it is up to them. One thing you should never do is to criticize them if they don't like you, not publicly anyway. It's fine to make negative comments about them to colleagues when you come off, but a really bad idea when you are in front of them. I saw a comedian do it once and that is where I learned the lesson. Yes, we had been quite tough on him, but to tell you the truth he wasn't that funny. In a desperate attempt to win us over, he resorted to a joke in such bad taste that it drew a collective groan of disapproval, which in turn led him to lose his temper with us! I guess he will never work in our town again.

This really is a case of applying the principle that the customer is always right.

BUILD YOUR SKILLS

If you decide to interact with your audience, avoid being too adventurous to begin with. Don't get me wrong, it's a great trick if you can pull it off and some of the most successful speakers are the ones who are able to really engage. The difficulty is you never know what you are going to get, so you need to be able to deal with any reaction. Some gentle introductions to audience interaction are listed below, before we look at this aspect in more detail:

- Ask for a show of hands. Make it something simple, so that people don't have to sit and debate the issue. Follow up by saying what the rough percentages are: 'So, it looks to me like about two-thirds of you feel like there aren't enough hours in the day to do your job.'

- Make a teasing statement. As long as the members of the audience know what it is you are doing, they will play along; just be careful not to upset anyone along the way. For example: 'I was speaking to your CEO earlier and he was telling me most of you feel as though you are paid way too much money for the hours you put in.'

- Try gentle humour, for example: 'When I was invited to speak here today and told that I'd be addressing an audience of the most talented personnel managers in the country, I couldn't resist the opportunity. Then, when I arrived, I found there was a double bonus, because you lot turned up as well.'

- Apply rhetorical ambiguity. This is when you ask a question where people feel as though they are probably not supposed to answer, but are not quite sure; for example: 'It's probably only me who feels this way, but I sometimes think we get sent too much e-mail!' Or turn it on its head (which will add some humour) 'I don't know about you, but sometimes I worry that I'm not getting enough e-mail!' When you use any kind of rhetoric, the idea is that the audience will understand and not answer, so don't stand there waiting for a reaction, just carry on with your speech. If there is a murmur of assent, or approval, let it go.

AUDIENCE INTERACTION

Selecting a victim

This strategy is not for the faint-hearted. A good practical demonstration, using a member of the audience, can win hearts and minds, but it is extremely risky. Don't ever do anything that will humiliate a member of the audience, unless you have had a regular slot on prime-time television as a professional comic for the past 10 years.

Real entertainers know not only how to work a room, but also how to select a member of the audience who is likely to play along. They never do this 'cold' by just pointing to a victim; instead they will build up to the selection, taking note of who is laughing, or engaged or outgoing. That's how dangerous it can be!

If you are going to do anything physical, you had better make sure in advance that your 'volunteers' are up to it. Choosing someone who is less able will cause embarrassment all round – the kind you are unlikely to recover from.

Finally, let me present you with a balanced view of audience interaction.

The case for

Using a member of the audience can take you closer to the crowd as a whole: if you do it skilfully, other people in the room will warm to you. Getting everyone to join in (perhaps to shout out a word or phrase on cue) is also bound to give a feeling of involvement to all present.

Really good handling of an audience is amusing, engaging and warm. It creates a fantastic atmosphere, makes you likeable and your messages memorable.

The case against

If you try but fail to deliver audience interaction, the results can be devastating. If you ask an open question and no one answers, or call for a volunteer to come up on stage and there isn't a taker, the embarrassment of everyone involved is palpable. Tricks, practical demonstrations or experiments that go wrong will not only fail to illustrate the point you were trying to make, they will actively contradict it. Someone who is uncomfortable with you on stage will make the audience squirm. Someone who is funnier than you will make you look stupid.

The conclusion

Love the members of your audience, but treat them with respect. Over time, think of gentle ways you might get them to join in. Plan these interventions carefully and always have a contingency plan in case they don't work out. Keep your moments of audience interaction as an optional extra. You can try them if things are going well, or wait for another day if the audience is tough.

Disaster case study
How not to handle an audience

Every now and again you just judge the audience wrongly, plain and simple. In my case, I had been booked to present a session on creativity to primary school teachers. So excited was I about the prospect of such engaging content to talk about, I forgot entirely to consider what the life, the experiences, the DNA of a primary school teacher was like.

There can't have been a single idea I presented that the teachers in the audience hadn't already thought of and implemented in their schools. Blank, bored and bemused faces stared back. All 200 of them.

Lesson learned? Well, given my time over again, I would think much more carefully about who these people are and what makes them tick. I would gather two or three guinea pigs together, listen to them and tell them what I intended to present, to get their input. And I would drink a whole 2-litre bottle of humility before going on stage.

Activity

For your next presentation, come up with a list of three rhetorical questions you could ask the audience, either as an opener, or in the body of the speech as a way of engaging with them. Choose the strongest one and try it out on the day.

SUMMARY

* There is nothing more important than the people in your audience. Handle them carefully – you need them on your side.

* Although a collection of individuals, audiences often display group behaviours. Winning over one can mean winning over all.

* Keep the members of your audience informed of what is going on. Make sure you manage their expectations at all times.

* If you decide you want to interact with audiences, begin with something simple and build up over time.

* Always be polite to the members of your audience – you never know when one of them might want to book you again.

QUESTION AND ANSWER SESSIONS

However you decide to handle audience interaction through the course of your speech, the part where you will often be forced to engage is in the question and answer session that has become so much a part of presentations. The first thing to say is this is not always necessary, we've just got into a kind of habit where speakers are expected to do it and audiences are expected to suffer it.

I say 'suffer' because there are so many times when we have to sit there and witness a stilted, or stage-managed question and answer session. The inevitable outcome of this is when you break for coffee, the thing uppermost in the minds of your audience is not the sparkling address you have just given, but the dull-as-ditchwater inquisition that followed it; not a good way to end.

THE DOWNSIDES

I know speakers who refuse point blank to do question and answer sessions, but not because they are scared. It is much more about having a limited time to put your message across, so you choose to use it wisely. If you have a lot of content to fit into an hour, why rush it so that you leave 10 minutes at the end for a pedestrian and often largely irrelevant, interaction?

Audiences often handle question and answer sessions badly as well. Either they are too shy to ask questions, resulting in that horrible silence as the speaker shifts from foot to foot, wondering if anyone will crack; or else the floor is opened to a loudmouth with a personal agenda.

So you see, the conventions of delivering a question and answer session need to be challenged. You really have to think hard about whether it will add anything to your address.

A word to the wise though. If you decide you are going to break with this modern tradition, it is probably better to front this up in a positive way at some point. Towards the end of your presentation, something like this might be appropriate: 'I've covered a lot of ground today and it may be that some of you have questions. In your packs, you'll find a copy of the slides I've used, along with some supporting notes, which should answer most of your queries. I'll also be around throughout the coffee break if there's anything you'd like to ask...' Then carry on with your presentation through to the end.

TIP

Never, never, never!

Never take questions during a presentation. It will hijack your content, spoil the flow, ruin your timings and throw you off balance. A focused discussion group is the place for questions and answers, not your carefully prepared speech.

TIPS FOR SUCCESS

If you do think it is a good idea to have a question and answer session, here are some handy tips to help you make the most of it:

* Don't be afraid. Lots of speakers are terrified that when they throw it open to the floor someone will ask a question they don't know the answer to. This really should not be a problem. First, you put the content together, so presumably have some insight into the subject you are talking about. If you don't know the exact answer to what they are asking, but feel it is legitimate to offer an educated guess, or your personal opinion, then do so, saying that's exactly what it is. If you have said what you think the answer is in your view, you can always throw this back to the questioner and ask 'Does that make sense? Is that what you think too?' If you really don't know the answer, then say so, but pledge to find out and make sure you do.

* Be prepared. If you have put the presentation together yourself, you will know the bits that are easy to explain and where the more complicated areas lie. Think about this when you are writing the content and you will probably be able to second guess the people in your audience; you will be able to spot the areas where they might want further clarification. They can be a right selfish lot, members of an audience. For example, if you are outlining plans to streamline a function of the company, they are less likely to ask about how that will affect the cost base, or the ongoing implications for customers and more likely to ask 'What will that mean for me?'

* Be even more prepared. When the moment arrives to let people in the audience have their say, we all know that terrible feeling of silence as tumbleweed blows through the auditorium. You

can avoid this in several ways. Agree up front with a plant (a trusted colleague), that he or she will get the ball rolling with the first question. Alternatively, whoever is hosting the session might be prepared to step in. In both of these cases, there is a good chance that the audience will spot your bit of advance stage management, but that's better than the silence. Failing this you can have a selection of pre-prepared questions that you introduce. Use one of the following to lead you in: 'Often when I talk about this subject, people ask me afterwards, why do you...?' Or 'When Kim first asked me to speak on this subject, she was keen to know the answer to...' If they still don't take the bait after this, you can legitimately wrap the thing up and all go for coffee, where, incidentally, you will be collared by a succession of people who have questions they would like you to answer.

- When a question is asked, you can give yourself some thinking time by repeating it back. This will also ensure that the rest of the audience has heard it. A technical point to note is that in large venues it is best to have a couple of roaming radio microphones. Get people to raise their hand if they have a question and dispatch one of your audio people to get a microphone to them, so the audience isn't wondering what's going on.

TIP

Mostly, audiences are not looking to catch you out. Now and again, if the mood is hostile, there will be someone who nominates themselves as a 'spokesperson for the people', even though in reality they're often only representing their own militant views.

Activity

In a small, controlled environment, such as a team meeting, set up an opportunity to rehearse your technique for questions and answers. Presenting a new idea to your colleagues and then asking for any questions will help to build your confidence for a bigger platform.

SUMMARY

● Having a question and answer session has become the norm, but you have every right to challenge this and opt out if you wish.

● Always keep questions and answers for the end of your presentation, otherwise it will interrupt your flow and make it hard for the audience to follow.

● To avoid an embarrassing silence have some questions already prepared that you can answer as a lead in to proper audience interaction.

● If you don't know the answer, say so – this is much better than trying to bluff your way out of the situation.

GETTING READY – SOME PRACTICAL ASPECTS

Most of the focus so far has been on responding to the brief, putting together a good presentation, making sure you are comfortable with it and coping with what you think you might have to deal with on the day. This isn't the only part of presenting though. There are also some practical but very important preparations to be made, well in advance if at all possible. Let's take a look at the things we need to do to get ready, starting with how you will look on the day.

APPEARANCE

This is really tricky to advise you on. A combination of political correctness and British politeness is supposed to prevent me from telling you that you look like a bag of washing, but to be honest, some of you do – you know who you are!

You haven't requested a makeover, so it's not for me to dress you, tell you how to have your hair or advise on make-up (especially for the fellas), but you should know by now that how you look is critical to the first impression you create. A 'look' that is inconsistent with your message will inevitably make life harder, especially in the first few critical moments of your presentation, when you are at your most nervous. If you show up to deliver a formal business presentation in a scruffy T-shirt and jeans, you had better have a good reason for doing so, or your audience will just be distracted.

Consider just two factors when deciding how you will look on the day. First, what will the audience expect? Second, what makes you comfortable?

If you are the CEO of a major corporation and have to make a speech at the company's AGM, then the expectation is you will be wearing a sober business suit. Women might accompany this with a plain blouse, guys with a shirt and tie. Hair will be neat and tidy. Shoes will be clean. This fits with the expectations of members of the audience and will, most likely, be how they are dressed, allowing you to deliver your content and focus attention solely on that. While you are doing this, the members of the audience are not thinking 'What on earth did he or she dress like that for?'

This is not necessarily about a level of formality, it is much more to do with appropriateness. Similarly, advertising agencies pitching to a new potential client often take along the account handler (known as the 'suit') and the art director (known as the 'creative'). You won't be surprised to learn that the 'suit' generally wears a suit, but the 'creative' should by rights be dressed in a ragbag assortment of clothes, have multiple piercings and/or tattoos and a Mohican haircut; alternatively, a long-haired, bearded hippy is also a common choice among the creative fraternity. Clients expect weirdness from their creatives, but not their business contacts.

All this is pretty logical, but it is not always the case that you have to mirror your audience in how you look. If you are conducting part of a training session, the audience may feel it's OK for them to turn up in jeans, as it's not a formal work day, but might still expect that you will be dressed for business.

Breaking with such traditions is fine, as long as there is a reason for doing it and that reason is not laziness! I once saw Bear Grylls, a mountaineer and British television presenter, conduct an entire address wearing his Everest-conquering gear, complete with ropes and other bits of mountaineering equipment. This was to an audience of teachers, not usually known for their sartorial elegance, but was perfectly acceptable, as he was talking about his assault on the summit and the lessons it taught him. Perfectly appropriate, it helped to make him memorable and reinforce his message.

Next comes comfort. I am not just talking about clothes that fit you, but also how they make you feel. Whatever the presentation, you need clothes that really are your size, not what you wish you were!

Then, when you are dressed, have a look in a full length mirror and decide 'Do I look good in this?' If you can answer 'yes' then you are comfortable, in the sense that you are at ease with your clothing. It is one less thing to worry about.

Some people just have a way with design and can carry off a stylish look without effort. If you are not like that, then find one and ask him or her for help in 'dressing' you.

Remember that a small number of well-tailored garments is better than a large collection of 'tat', so splash out on your 'stage wear' and make yourself feel good.

Real power dressing

Laurence was Sales Director of a company manufacturing window blinds and curtains.

While liaising with a major supplier over the launch of a new range of fabrics he was called to an important meeting with the supplier and felt he should make the effort to dress appropriately.

On the day, he turned up wearing an immaculate suit, tailored from the new curtain material. That's how to power dress!

EQUIPMENT

Aside from what you are wearing, the checklist of what to take to a presentation will depend on the sort of gig it is. An internal company meeting, attended by a handful of your peers, won't need the same amount of equipment as a conference address to a room of 200 guests.

When you are really good at presentations, you will just be able to turn up on your own, confident in your ability and prepared to stand and talk off the cuff for however long is required. As your skills improve, you will find that a few well-constructed cue cards in your jacket pocket or handbag will provide all the insurance policy you need. Other than that, you will be happy to rely on your innate ability.

At the other end of the spectrum, where you have been booked to conduct a full-day seminar on your specialist subject, with all the attendant bells and whistles that are part of the modern presentation kit, you might decide to carry more gear than a U2 world tour.

Certainly, with unfamiliar venues and people you may not have dealt with until now, employing a belt and braces approach is a good idea. Whatever they have told you they can supply, take it as read that they are lying; then you will be prepared for anything. I have never gone quite so far as taking my own flipchart easel, but many times I have taken spare pads with me and fresh new felt pens are a must, as it is a golden rule that any hotel's conference facility only contains pens with enough ink left to write up the title of a chart.

If PowerPoint is your thing, then obviously the least you need to do is carry a set of the slides with you in electronic format. If you trust the contact at the conference facility, you can arrange to e-mail the presentation in advance, so that your contact can load it up for you, ready to go when you arrive.

Good idea

Rather than just relying on a single source for your slides, take a back-up copy with you on a memory stick. You can also e-mail a version to your own web mail account, so that you can pick this up from any computer once you arrive at the venue.

A step up from here is also to load your presentation onto a laptop, taking the memory stick as well, just in case. Devices are getting smaller all the time; if you cannot drive the presentation from your phone by the time you are reading this, it won't be long before you can. Power might be an issue, so take items that are fully charged, have spare batteries where appropriate and take an electrical extension lead with multiple points to plug into. Strong parcel or gaffer tape is also a must, as you might have to set up some way from an electrical point and tape down any trailing wires.

Good idea

If you are being called on to do more and more presentations, at remote venues, with facilities you can never be sure of, then invest in a data projector. These are now much cheaper than they used to be. If you do this and also take along the multiple versions of your slides, the only thing the venue will need to provide is a blank wall to project onto, which by coincidence, is the one item I'm suggesting you don't have to take.

When it comes to handouts and resources (any props, prompts, paper exercises or physical kit that you need to distribute), take more copies than you need. The extra 'wasted' cost is worth it, as insurance against not having enough, and if you are clever you will find a way of reusing the materials at a later date. Expecting the venue's staff to be able to photocopy any extras is a dangerous game. Even if they can and they deliver them to your presentation suite before you get started, it is still bound to cost you dearly.

Assembling a kit of stationery items is useful. You never know when you are going to need the following:

- stapler – (having checked it is fully loaded);

- pencils, sharpener and eraser;

- pens;

- hole punch and treasury tags;

- rule;

- reusable adhesive putty and masking tape (for attaching flipcharts to walls).

Coming up is advice on how to compile a delivery schedule for each presentation. When you have done this, you should add all your regular items of equipment, as a tick-box checklist. Use the template each time your prepare a presentation. It is better to take more than you think you will need.

When you don't have any gigs lined up for a while, store all your presentation kit together, so that you don't have to search round the house for the component parts. Plastic storage boxes that collapse down flat are available at good DIY stores and are ideal for carting this sort of stuff around in. It also means that after you have set up at the venue you can fold the boxes away.

As an aside, when you are self-contained like this, it means shifting and carrying quite a lot of kit. Make sure you check in advance with hotels and conference facilities that you can park close to where you will be setting up. This is particularly important in city centre venues, where parking restrictions might apply.

Once you have set up all the technical kit, make sure you tidy anything else away, out of sight, so your audience cannot see what you have brought. Use a long table, positioned behind where you will stand to lay out any giveaways or handouts and put them in the order you will come across them in the presentation. There's nothing worse than juggling bits of paper, or not being able to find the handout you are looking for.

The hardware you might need will vary from one presentation to another, but the constant in all of this is the confidence you feel from being well prepared. The more variables there are, the more important it is to control the things you can. With forethought, planning and a comprehensive kit of parts, you will always look and feel like a professional. It is a good idea to make a checklist for the day. Table 16.1 gives a useful example.

Table 16.1 Checklist for PowerPoint presentations

Equipment/Things to do	Check
Have I e-mailed the presentation to my contact?	
Have I charged my laptop?	
Have I got:	
a set of slides in electronic format?	
a memory stick of the presentaiton?	
mains and connecting leads?	
an electrical extension lead?	
strong parcel or gaffer tape?	
printed handouts of the presentation?	
the name and contact number of the venue's technical person, for set up?	
Have I checked where I can park?	

Activity

Make your own presentation checklist, taking the suggestions from this chapter as a starting point and adding any extra items that are specific to your own sphere. Buy any outstanding items and keep them all together as part of your kit.

SUMMARY

● Don't neglect the details of preparation, including how you will look on the day and what you will take with you.

● Dress appropriately and comfortably, then you can focus on the job in hand instead of worrying about what you are wearing.

● Assemble your own presentation kit. Keep all the items together, with a checklist, to tick off what is needed for each speech.

● Always take more handouts and resources than you need. It increases your confidence if you are prepared for anything and it makes you look more professional.

● If you are doing lots of presentations, it is worth investing in the technical kit you need – that way you can be guaranteed it will be working.

AS THE MOMENT APPROACHES

When the day of the presentation finally arrives, I hope it will dawn with you feeling a mixture of excitement, anticipation and a few nervous moments (which are good for keeping you sharp).

Here we look at the lead-up to your address, as well as examining some strategies for what to do when things don't quite go to plan. Armed with this knowledge, nothing can stop you.

THE FINAL COUNTDOWN

I have purposely not put any timescale on the countdown to your presentation, simply because the timescales for different presentations can be so variable. Instead, I have just given a sequence of events, adding here and there the ideal amount of time for a particular stage:

- Preparation. This can involve anything from the receipt of a full written brief to an off-the-cuff request to speak. Whatever its form, this is the stage where you need to consider what the task is, who the audience will be and how you will deliver against the set objective.

● Writing. If you are very good at speeches and have been asked to talk on your specialist subject, a few sketched notes will act as a sufficient aide-memoire to the words you have probably spoken a thousand times before. At the other end of the spectrum, when you have been asked to deliver new content you may not be so familiar with, the writing stage is critical. Bear this in mind, as it will have an impact on how much time you need.

● Rehearsal. If you want to get better, then get to know your material with full confidence, so you have more chance of concentrating on the 'performance'. Ideally, you should be fully rehearsed the day before you are due to present. My own preference is to have a final run through at home, or in the car on the way to the event just to double-check I know what I am going to say. After that I leave it alone. I have seen speakers sitting in a row on a platform, waiting for their turn and nervously shuffling through pages of notes. It's not a good look and betrays their lack of confidence.

● Familiarization. This is the process I think of as the great 'nerve calmer'. Get to the venue with plenty of time to spare. Before a major presentation, it is unlikely you will be able to focus on any other pressing task, so devote yourself wholly to this issue – the e-mail inbox will wait. Use the time before the presentation to get familiar with the layout of the room. Talk to the venue's technical people, find out what they expect and what they can offer. Check with your host on the detail of timings, how you will be announced and by whom. If you have had a chance to do all this in advance, then there is still no excuse for not arriving early. It can offer all sorts of benefits. You might pick up on some detail that you can work into your opening, about the venue itself or the local area. You might be able to meet some delegates in advance and sharing what they tell you with the wider audience can be a great way of engaging with the whole group. Or you may spend the time getting to know the other speakers or your host, all of which could lead to you being 'booked' again in the future.

* Go with the flow. Now is not the time to be having a tantrum about the fact the lectern microphone is set at the wrong height, or that there were no puppies in your dressing room, as you had specified! It is too late; you just have to go with what is in front of you. In fact, in many ways the ability to be unfazed by anything the day might throw at you is the mark of a true professional. Any prima-donna-like foot stamping, which I might say you are fully entitled to do, should have been done during the lead-up to today.

* Be charming and relaxed. Ha! Yeah, that's easy to say isn't it? Quite naturally, as the moment approaches, you will become increasingly nervous, but often your hosts want to know they have booked the right man or woman, so pacing up and down and proclaiming loudly 'They always make me really nervous, these things!' is not likely to fill them (or you) with oodles of confidence. When you are up there on stage it is a bit like putting on an act, so add to your case for an Oscar by starting the process the minute you arrive at the venue.

* Showtime. Immediately prior to being announced is the time when your heart will probably be beating fastest. If you have followed the golden rules of preparation and really nailed that opening, you will be fine, just remember that. Keep smiling, look confident – of course you can! – approach the podium, take your time and deliver that killer first line. After that it's easy, I promise you.

I WASN'T EXPECTING THAT!

Anyone who has done the rounds on the speaker circuit will tell you the same thing: if it can go wrong, it will. This is rather cold comfort for the rookie, nervous presenter who is not only terrified of getting up there, but also of things going wrong.

Worst of all is when something happens that you were not expecting; then you really do have to think on your feet. Let's attempt to eradicate some of those situations by having a look at the common issues that arise.

Equipment meltdown

The most common thing to go wrong with presentations is the hardware. Do some basic checks when you get to the venue and make sure things are working the way you want them to.

With PowerPoint, ensure that it is loaded up and ready to go. Flick through the slides in a dummy run and check them against your notes. If you are really afraid of the technology crashing, take along a hard copy of the slides you can present from, so that the audience will still get something of what you had intended. Alternatively, rely less on the gift of PowerPoint in the writing stage.

If you are faced with equipment meltdown, stay on the front foot as much as is humanly possible – just shrug, say it would have been nice to have the accompanying visuals, but it's no big deal. Don't keep referring wistfully to how much more wonderful this experience would have been if only the audience had been able to see slide 8, or 12, or 176; it's gone, let it go.

If you are using a flipchart make sure the easel is not wobbling and that you have sufficient pens.

The sky is falling

Call it an act of God or some such thing, but occasionally, during your presentation, you are faced with something entirely unexpected. I once had a ceiling tile cave in at the back of the room. It didn't hit anyone, but the noise it made caused a bit of a commotion. Fire alarms going off is more common than you would think. I have often wished I could make this happen with a remote control, during a presentation that's going badly! Delegates fainting, waiters wandering in and walking across your eye-line, shouts, laughter, or the sound of ecstasy from the room next door; you name it, it can happen. Take it as it comes. If it is minor, ignore it. If not, deal with it as quickly as possible and move on.

Mis-communication

I am a bit loathe to put this in as a heading, but I suppose I have to as it is so commonplace. Or is it? Usually the 'breakdown in communication' is a universal excuse to cover up for the fact that someone screwed up. It is still a good idea to try and eradicate it, by making sure that the communications that are issued from *your* end are clear, concise and unequivocal.

You don't have to be officious when you discuss your requirements as a speaker, but it's fine to be firm. Try to confirm everything in writing and ask that the organizers acknowledge what you have sent them. I always find it a great help if the organisation you are presenting to nominates a project manager, someone who will oversee all your requirements. You cannot force them to do this, but you can at least ask for a point of contact who will guide you on the day of the presentation itself.

Summarizing all the key information about a presentation is a good way of ensuring that communication happens effectively. Sometimes you will be sent this information in the form of a delivery schedule by whoever has booked you, but if not you need to be proactive: compile your own and send it to key people at the venue. An example is shown in Figure 17.1.

Delivery schedule

Client:	Health Systems plc
Venue:	Western House Brighton Street Wolford W1 VCX
Date & time:	14.12.2011 – 09:30
Contact:	Richard Lazarus 0661 4661 (office) 07476 112 (mobile)
Type of event:	National sales conference
Speaker requirements:	Laptop Data projector PowerPoint Flipchart & pens
Room layout:	'Cabaret' style (10 delegates per table)

Figure 17.1 Sample delivery schedule

Activity

Draw up a delivery schedule. You can base it on the example shown if you wish. When you use it in practice, be sure to number and date each version, so if the situation changes, at either end, you can be certain both parties are working off the same sheet.

SUMMARY

- Go through the stages of preparation fully and you will feel confident about what you are going to present.

- Arrive early. It gives you a chance to familiarize yourself with the venue and to settle in.

- Be prepared for things going wrong, they sometimes do and it is the sign of a professional presenter if you can rise above this.

- Ensure that all your communication prior to the event is clear and unambiguous, to avoid too many surprises on the day.

STRIPPED BARE

There is a level of presentation skill we all aspire to, being able to stand before an audience without any tools, notes or cues and deliver a seamless address without missing a beat. Very few master this advanced technique, but it is possible with planning and practice.

This chapter looks at the art of presenting, stripped bare. We'll examine the risks and the benefits as well as considering how it can be achieved. Let's begin though by looking at a rationale for taking the risk, what are the 'fors' and 'againsts'?

Why not?

For most of us the thought of having nothing to fall back on when we are presenting is intimidating to say the least, but why is that? We already know that if we trace the fear of presentations back to its roots, the one thing we are most scared of is looking foolish. In front of our peers or customers we are afraid of drying up, saying the wrong thing entirely, losing our thread and generally coming across as incompetent. There is the added fear that without structure our presentation won't keep to time or stay on message.

Why?

Taking a more positive stance, the main reasons for choosing to deliver in this way are the counterpoint to the risks. An audience can recognize how difficult a task it is to deliver without accompaniment and this in itself is an impressive feat. It signals that you are brave, passionate and accomplished; it says you are sufficiently sure of your ground to not need any 'outside' help. Paradoxically perhaps, they are more likely to be forgiving of 'mistakes' which is a factor which immediately starts to ameliorate some of the risk. If things do seem to go a little off script they will make allowances for this, balancing it against the fact that what they are getting is genuinely 100% you.

OVERCOMING THE FEAR OF EXPOSURE

Sitting having coffee with friends most of us wouldn't hesitate to tell a story which illustrated the topic under discussion and a presentation stripped bare is simply a scaled up version of this. What underlies our fear is in fact illogical, we are afraid we won't be able to deliver and yet we do it all the time, the only difference is the size and make up of the audience.

Perceptions of audiences

As we have already discovered in Chapter 2, once an audience reaches a certain size the addition of extra people makes no real difference. In the coffee scenario we feel comfortable 'holding court' with perhaps up to a dozen people. It can be just as embarrassing making a gaffe in front of that many as an audience of 100 so the numbers are not really important.

There is a point at which an audience, in the eyes of a nervous presenter, becomes an amorphous mass (some think of it as a 'baying mob' but that's just a matter of interpretation!). The reality is audiences are made up of *individuals* and if we think of presenting to one person, the whole task gets easier.

Expectation

Similarly, audiences can be as varied as the people in them and judging the situation in advance is one of the toughest jobs we face. There is a world of difference between proposing a toast at a family occasion and addressing the staff at the annual conference. Their issues are not the same, nor is their 'advance engagement'. What we are trying to define here is 'audience readiness', how prepared are they for what you are going to say and what is their level of 'sympathy' with your cause? In the former case it is a social gathering where no one wants to see you fail; they are on your side before you open your mouth. The latter scenario is much more volatile, maybe you've had a good year and are going to announce that everyone is to get a bonus, or more likely you might have to deliver some tough messages.

Flying solo, without the aid of the usual presentation support mechanisms can be even more powerful in a situation which is a little adversarial. We recognize that there are risks, but winning an audience over might be better done by presenting yourself as open and vulnerable than by hiding behind a lectern and a couple of dozen Power Points.

WHAT WILL I ACHIEVE?

If you are still not convinced of the benefits of presenting this way, here are some of the positives which might help to sway your view.

- **Becoming a consummate professional** Whatever it is you say, this is only a small part of a presentation. Often style has a way of complementing substance (it is rarely, if ever a substitute!) Standing alone on a stage signals your self-confidence to an audience, it says 'look, this is me and this is what I have to say'. Confidence is a trait which is much better judged from the outside than the inside. We may not be feeling at our most bullish, but if we can pull off a tolerable performance without too many glitches, other people will perceive us as competent.

- **Perception becomes reality** Performers and presenters who have had years of experience often have 'pre-match nerves' it's part of the territory. However, get enough 'stage time' in and the confidence you were *faking* a few months ago will start to turn into the feeling you really can do this!

Alan – Consultant Engineer

'I suppose I could say there was a tipping point, it's just I'm not sure when it occurred. I was always nervous before I got up to speak, but after about a year of doing it regularly someone came up afterwards and said "how come you're so at ease when you're on stage?". It brought me up short and only when I looked back over that period of time did I realize how much more relaxed I really was'

We have all heard the expression 'building confidence' and that is exactly what happens. Think about any skill you have mastered and consider the process which took you there. Your first driving lesson was probably difficult, remembering all those different things which needed to be done to drive safely. A few years on and this becomes second nature. *Familiarity* builds confidence so when you get to a point where being 'on stage' is nothing out of the ordinary you will no longer be put off by microphones, lecterns or large groups of people staring at you! Confidence *builds*, you simply have to put in the hours.

PREPARING TO SUCCEED

Nothing to lose

What's the worst that can happen? You probably have a long list of disaster scenarios in your head but they are unlikely to come to pass if a bit of thought and preparation goes into the project. Sometimes nervous presenters have an image of perfection in their heads and if they don't live up to this they consider it a failure.

An audience is just people, they know things go wrong, they are aware of the difficulties of presentations and they rarely expect perfection. If the microphone fails, don't crumple into a heap, say something like 'if you listen carefully now you'll hear the sound of one of our technicians being taken out and flogged!'

Sometimes a bit of vulnerability goes a long way with an audience, it shows you are human. Treat glitches with good humour, don't be tempted to criticize and have an attitude which says, 'let's carry on regardless.' Resilience can be an appealing trait too.

Safety-nets can be built in to everything you do and if something happens which you really didn't anticipate treat it as a learning experience. The confidence building we have just talked of is shored up by having dealt with some difficult scenarios. Technical failure, fire alarms going off or strangers walking into the room looking lost. When you have handled these things once, they will never put you off again.

Develop spontaneity

Although presenting without any supporting aids can be intimidating at first, it is a great way of putting yourself on the spot. Although this is the reason so few people are prepared to attempt it, what you do find quite quickly is how to deal with the unexpected, you're forced into it.

Just as a great comedian becomes a master of the ad lib, so you too get to a stage where you are able to handle pretty much anything which comes your way. Not only is this a great skill to acquire but it also has the added benefit of high level audience engagement. Don't we all love to see someone triumph over adversity?

Adult content

'As an after dinner speaker I often included stories which could best be described as "adult". Once I stood up to speak at an early evening event and noticed some children in the audience, I opened by saying "Some of my anecdotes are for grown-ups only, so my worst fear before a speech is to spot a can of soda and a packet of M & M's!" I then went on to tell the original stories, sanitized for a general audience and as I struggled through, with the adults filling in the gaps for themselves, they loved watching the process unfold.'

ADVANCED MEMORY TIPS

One of the greatest fears with this kind of venture is that we will stand in front of an expectant audience and forget everything we intended to say. Here, as reinforcement of what we have already outlined in Chapters 4 and 9 are some *extra* memory techniques.

Work the material

If you have left yourself sufficient preparation time for your speech you should have it developed and written well in advance. This gives you the luxury of running some of it past an audience. I've mentioned finding a trusted colleague or friend who would be prepared to listen and give you feedback and in itself this is no bad idea. However, it lacks the authenticity of a *real* audience. You have already prompted your 'listener' and they are probably desperate to give you *positive* feedback.

Another advanced technique is to take parts of the speech and 'slip them into conversation'. This can be particularly useful if you are attempting humour. Clearly you can only do this with snatches of the speech but it gives you a chance for a try-out in a safe environment. If people laugh you can be confident in keeping those lines in, if it's more serious subject matter, try to gauge a reaction in terms of engagement.

Performance is rehearsal

Some speeches we make are a one-off but there are also instances where we can use the content time and time again. We re-visit practical examples of this shortly in 'creating standard material'. Let us say you are asked to present on your specialist subject, for the sake of argument 'using social media to win more business'. The first time you deliver it you may be too nervous to take much account of audience reaction, but over time as the presentation flows more smoothly you should get a sense of the things that generally go down well and the parts which are less engaging. Count this process as a rehearsal for the next time you have to deliver and you will improve with each occasion.

Use a mnemonic

The three part rule of constructing a speech applies more than ever when you are going to be unscripted. Giving each of these sections its own key word is a way of leading you in. Save for the odd politician, most of us can remember three words! Using alliteration might help but so can making up a word.

A vital cue

The topic of the presentation is in-car satellite navigation. The three vital messages are the interchangeable *voices* you can now get for your satnav, the *invention* of the technology and an illustrative story about *people* using it incorrectly. Here the key words are 'voices', 'invention' and 'people'. By remembering V.I.P. the outline of the speech is fixed in your head.

The kitchen is not your stage

Wherever you choose to rehearse, driving in the car, while running on the treadmill, or when making a cup of tea none of it will ever simulate the feeling we get when we're standing up in front of the real live audience. This is one of the reasons for emphasizing repetition in the rehearsal process. No matter how well you think you know it an extra run through will be of benefit. The only rule is to have a cut off point around an hour before you are due to speak so you have time to gather yourself together. As I have already said, rehearsing right up to the point when you are announced can increase anxiety and be more of a hindrance than a help.

You will forget!

In coaching hundreds of speakers over many years, the question they most often ask is 'but what happens if I do forget something?' The answer is always the same, 'you will!' The real issue from a professional presentational point of view is whether or not the audience will know. Once we accept there is a likelihood we will forget, it removes some of the pressure and as long as we can keep going no one but us will ever know.

They don't know what you're going to say!

CREATING STANDARD MATERIAL

We are familiar with the feelings of nervousness which occur when first standing up to speak, but in the main these subside quickly once we're into the flow. This is why I have suggested constructing a standard opening which can be adapted to different circumstances. Apart from saving the time and trouble of thinking of a new beginning for each speech, it will get you over the early nerves. By the same token I have recommended building up a collection of stories to fall back on. Over time you can develop a bank of content relevant to your industry or job role. Universal stories like our struggle with technology, the pace of change in business or managing information overload will always come in handy and can sometimes be 'fed in' at an appropriate moment. Having a store of stories also gives you some leeway when it comes to timing: if you think you're going to fall short of your allotted slot, you can 'fill' with an appropriate anecdote – just make sure it's relevant.

How to open

In Chapter 11 I outlined the importance of a strong opening and this is never more so than when you are going to go unscripted. There are dozens of ways you can begin a speech and whichever you choose the advice is the same as before, make sure you know it off by heart. Be true to your personality, don't flatter or flannel if you haven't got anything genuinely good to say but if you truly have had a positive experience at this event or venue in the past it's a good strong way of opening. Here are 3 examples.

1 When x asked me if I'd come and speak to you today I jumped at the chance, otherwise I'd be sitting at home watching daytime television!

2 One of the difficulties we all face in business today is having too much time on our hands and not enough to do.

3 I always love coming to (name of town) because it reminds me of (anecdote about previous visit).

We have talked before about the benefits of a story which is self-deprecating. This is one of my personal favourites – it helps that it is true.

'The last time I did this was at a wedding and afterwards a woman approached me and said, "When they announced it was time for the speeches my heart sank!". I quickly interjected and said I was sorry if it had spoiled her day. "Oh no", she replied, "you weren't nearly as boring as I thought you were going to be!"

It is perhaps my best testimonial so far.'

With plenty of experience we develop a kind of filing system in our heads where we store the content which we have collected over a period of time. This can then be mixed and matched to create new presentations, opening with a line about the current economic conditions, telling a story about the effects of organizational culture, following this with 3 main points about the changes we all face in the workplace and wrapping up with an amusing anecdote about a customer service interaction.

Just because you have read a chapter about advanced level presentation skills this doesn't mean it will take away all the fears of presenting 'unplugged': it is only practice which will do this. Start small, don't be too ambitious at first, know where you are going, have a back-up plan (some cue cards in your pocket as an insurance policy) and be both human and yourself. After that it's easy.

SUMMARY

* Preparation is the key to success.

* Confidence builds in direct proportion to time spent 'on stage'.

* Do your best to remember, don't fret if you forget.

* Presenting without aids is hard, but the rewards are worth it.

ADVANCED INTERACTIVITY

There is a degree of interactivity in *all* presentations and we examined the basics of this in Chapter 14. You speak, they listen, it's sort of interactive. However, recent technological developments have led us to realize that rich, real time interactivity can now be a part of any address. It has caused us to think again about relating to audiences and getting feedback. There is now an opportunity for *advanced* interactivity.

In this chapter we will look at more ways we can involve our audience with techniques as old as the Q & A, through to instant reaction via a Twitter feed. We will consider the pluses and minuses as well as the benefits and examine ways of controlling the process so you don't cede the power of your presentation to a member of the audience.

THE TROUBLE WITH FEEDBACK

For most people in business the word 'feedback' is steeped in negativity. if we hear the phrase 'can you come into my office, I want to give you some feedback' the immediate reaction of a majority of people is 'what have I done wrong?' And yet we know that logic dictates we can only improve our own performance if we are able to get a real sense of what an audience thinks. Aside from the potential for praise or criticism it is an opportunity to check understanding; is their interpretation of our message the same as our original intention? Have we missed anything? Was the style and complexity right?

Feedback forms (sometimes called 'happy sheets') are the bane of most presenters' lives too. If the assembled throng have been asked to comment on our performance, the first reaction for most of us is to riffle through looking for the negatives. Often a single unhappy 'customer' can undo all the good of a hundred who were delighted.

Try to see feedback as your friend, a way of checking not only that today went okay, but for shaping tomorrow too.

IS IT DANGEROUS?

Many people are fearful of asking an audience's opinion because they don't want to hear the bad news. This is short-sighted as presentations shouldn't be seen as a survival course where you do your bit and hope to get off the stage unscathed, instead they are a real and vital opportunity to make a connection.

If interactivity can be judged to be 'dangerous' it is only because we cannot predict with certainty the reaction we will get. However, with forethought and planning much can be done to militate against a potential disaster.

IS IT HELPFUL?

If you think your message is significant enough to want people to remember it then 'engagement' is an imperative. The sure fire way of doing this is to think of the presentation as a two-way street, not something where you simply hector them with your views. This can only be done through some form of interaction. Let's examine some ways of executing this.

A RANGE OF INTERACTIVE TECHNIQUES

The first thing to say about getting a response is it is much easier if there is safety in numbers. If you ask the audience 'does anyone have an example of poor communication they can share with us?' it entails a single individual having the courage to suddenly turn themselves into 'presenter'. Contrast this with an example where you ask for collective choice, e.g. 'give me a cheer if you prefer the Blackberry....now give me a cheer if you'd rather have an iPhone'. Use this or the simple 'show of hands' I talked about in chapter 14. Whatever the reaction, you can usually create a fitting quip.

1. Ask questions

I've talked about one of the simplest ways of drawing an audience towards you: ask them a question, then yours is not the only voice that's heard. I'd caution once again that you are careful with this technique. Firstly, make sure it's planned. An off-the-cuff question might seem like a good idea but could lead you down a blind alley. Unless you have good reason to, don't ask a question too early in the presentation (see the upcoming section 'warming them up to interactivity'). Always keep the possible answers as simple as you can: tying an audience member up in knots will work against you in the engagement stakes.

Think ahead

An important part of questioning is being prepared for *any* response. Let us say you are speaking on 'How to get the best out of e-mail' and you ask the following question:

'How do we think we might use e-mail better?'

What do you do if you get any of the following?

a No response at all

b A range of helpful suggestions

c A maverick answer, for example 'we should ban all e-mail from now on'

Unless you prepare yourself for a wide range of responses (including complete silence) you risk being thrown off track, so make sure you have a follow up strategy for each set of circumstances.

If you feel a more structured level of interaction is required then refer back to the advice on setting up a formal Q & A session at the end of your speech.

2. Use a voting system

Large conference facilities can supply a sophisticated electronic voting system where delegates press a number on a key pad to respond to a range of options you have presented them with. This information is instantly collated and projected onto a PowerPoint slide. Alternatively you can just ask for a quick vote. It is not the *complexity* which matters, but the fact you have asked for an opinion in a non-intimidating way. A fun way of doing this is to have A4 cards printed with a red hand on one side and a green one on the other, the audience then displays agreement or dissent to your idea by 'showing' the side which matches their opinion.

Think carefully when you are compiling your questions if you want to avoid confusion. The 'keep it simple' rule applies.

3. Advance set up

Sometimes you can get your audience to do some work beforehand. If you are holding an internal company conference the delegate list will be compiled well in advance and so will the programme of topics. You can e-mail something to the delegates before your speech to prompt their thoughts. This helps to manage their expectation and act as a catalyst on the day, so you won't be starting from 'cold'. Here is an example:

The big 3!

'At next week's conference I will be talking about our sales effort next year. My presentation will be called "The big 3" because I believe there are 3 key things we will need to do to meet our targets. But maybe I'm wrong, so what are your big 3? Bring them along on the day and we'll have an opportunity to share our ideas.'

You may not have sufficient time or insider knowledge for this, but a simplified version might be to have 'burning question' cards in the registration area. As guests arrive your team can be prompted to ask them to fill these out and leave them in a box. This gives you the chance to see their issues ahead of your speech and it takes the pressure off individuals who may not want to raise their hand and ask out loud.

4. Post match analysis

Feedback often comes in what has become known as 'happy sheets', but rather than having this as a 'tick box' exercise try to think creatively. By now you know the importance of understanding an audience and one thing which is common to most people is a desire to get away when an event has finished; many will have a long commute or may want to return to their desks to answer the never ending e-mail stream. The last thing most people want to do is fill out a detailed questionnaire about your presentation.

How then do we get away from just having a few random ticks on a sheet of paper? One way of doing this is to ask delegates for 'one word feedback', an open exercise where they can write anything they like to describe the session (from experience, many take the time to write longer comments). During a longer event, don't save the feedback right for the end. Prior to afternoon coffee you can prompt delegates to fill in their feedback during the break. You can use the line 'if you'd like to get ahead of the game, please feel free to fill in your feedback forms over coffee. If you're concerned we haven't yet finished, I can tell you I don't get any better than this!' It is much more likely you will get richer, more detailed comments if people don't feel under pressure to 'hit the road'.

If at all possible, you should try to follow up on feedback so people don't feel it was a waste of time. Ask for suggestions as well as assessment or critique and e-mail or contact those who have taken the time to pass comment.

5. Use a

Social media has many uses. For lots of people it is simply a fun way of keeping in touch with friends, but this same technology can be employed for real time interaction. Many large conferences now use a specific hash tag (#) on Twitter related to the event. Whoever posts either from a laptop or smart phone the thread of comment can be seen by other delegates. This can be a great way of capturing audience opinion over the course of a day, or even during a specific speech.

You may need some advance set-up to advise delegates this tool will be used and an explanation at the start of the day for those who are not familiar with the technology, but it is well worth it in terms of quality interaction.

The larger the audience, the less likely people are to raise a hand to forward their point of view: however, using social media you can get instant responses to what you are saying.

'I have outlined our customer charter based on what we currently think, but maybe there's something missing? Pair up with the person next to you, have a chat for the next 5 minutes and see if you can come up with anything new, then post it at #kpconference and we'll take a look at a selection of the suggestions.'

6. Hang around and chat

This seems obvious but many presenters dash for the door the minute they finish, just in case they get 'collared' by someone who took issue with what was said. Where possible, use the less formal time after a presentation to gather the views of audience members. This is harder if you are last on stage at a conference, but if you are guest speaker at an evening event for a professional body, ask that you go on first and have the buffet supper afterwards. This gives people a chance to approach you and discuss their feelings.

7. Play the long game

We live in such an instantaneous world we have come to expect everything to happen right now! It is true that after most events or speeches there is a law of diminishing returns once they have finished. People tend to give a 'knee-jerk' reaction and then move on to the next thing. However, you may be in a situation where you conduct a quarterly address to colleagues. Under these circumstances it is useful to keep an open dialogue going during the time *between* events. In this way you can show your audience you have listened to their suggestions or concerns, followed up afterwards and amended your actions to take account of what they said.

One reason many people dislike feedback is they see it as a 'vanity' exercise on the part of the speaker. If instead you turn it into a 'conversation' over a longer period, they will be much more likely to stay engaged with the process and offer their thoughts more readily.

WARMING THEM UP TO INTERACTIVITY

We know audiences can often be reserved, particularly early in the day when they haven't been warmed up, and this will limit their propensity to join in, which makes interactivity a bit difficult. The way you treat them can have a big effect here: if they feel they are being cajoled or even intimidated into a response they may back off even more.

Use simple techniques to get them on your side. Firstly, don't scare them by being too 'in their face'. Lead in gently and get them on your side before you attempt the riskier aspects of presenting. We've already considered the difficulties of getting a volunteer on stage from a cold start; they need to trust you first, even to like you. Then and only then can you hope to get a good response to your attempted interaction. Remove barriers as much as possible, don't hide behind a lectern or a wad of notes, try to use open gestures with your hands to 'welcome them in' and smile as much as is reasonable! Put some energy into your performance, look and act passionate and make it appear that you are enjoying yourself – they are much more likely to engage then. When it comes to language, keep it informal and remember to use lots of inclusive phrases, things like 'we all hate poor customer service, don't we?', or 'which of us hasn't felt like getting on our soapbox from time to time?' While we're on this subject, rhetorical questions like these are fine, but take the earlier advice when it comes to a proper question to which you expect an answer and remember the golden rule, keep it simple.

By people's body language we are often able to tell how relaxed they are in our company, so keep aware of this while you are speaking and wait for the audience to be ready for interactivity before you thrust it upon them.

Great speakers involve the people they address and as with many techniques we get better at doing this over time. Expect the unexpected and build your experience of interaction.

SUMMARY

● Interactivity is the best way of engaging an audience.

● Welcome feedback, it helps you develop better presentations.

● Treat your audience with respect, don't intimidate them.

● Choose a method you know will work, whether simple voting or complex interaction.

PROGRESS REPORT

I have deliberately steered away from setting targets in this book. Yes, goal setting is important, but how you do that is up to you. Base it on where you are now, how far you want to travel and how fast.

All this chapter does is suggest some ways you can monitor your progress. Seeking other people's opinion will be a large part of this, but we are in an area of subjectivity, so take as wide a range of measures as possible to try and get a realistic perspective on how you are doing.

YOU ARE THE BEST JUDGE

For most things in life, we can usually tell when we have done well or badly. If you play sport, you know the instant you leave the field of play whether you have had a good game or not. The same is true if you make a presentation. Get into the habit of thinking of your presentation as three separate speeches. Before you go on stage, visualize what it will be like; second, do the speech itself ; and third, look back on how it actually was. If you think about the differences between your expectations, your experience and your hindsight you can begin to understand where the gaps are from what you planned, to what you delivered, to what the audience received.

VIDEO AND REVIEW

Lots of professional conference facilities now have the technology on hand to be able to film sessions, so when you get the chance try to make sure yours is captured. This is not about narcissism; it is only so you have the opportunity to see yourself as others see you.

Quickly put aside your discomfort over how you look and sound and instead try to focus objectively on your performance as a whole. When did you rush things too much? At what point did the audience laugh and why? How could you edit the content down to make it even tighter? These are the sort of questions you should be trying to answer.

When you have answered them, by all means go back to the subject of how you appear and the way your voice comes across, but see it from the audience's point of view. Are you engaging, interesting and entertaining? If you have still got some work to do, try to make the changes over time, then get yourself filmed again, so you can start the loop of continuous improvement.

GOOD FRIENDS VERSUS JEALOUS PEERS

Be careful who you listen to. Presenting badly is a blow to the confidence and a dent in your ego. For this reason, the people who like you might want to protect you from the truth. They will tell you it was fine, when really it wasn't.

The other side of the coin is the resentful colleague who recognizes you did a good job, but will never admit it. Quite often there is a subtlety to the criticism you might face from these people. They are unlikely to be openly hostile, but might try to undermine you, by saying a few people at the back were yawning or someone commented your slides seemed a bit over-complicated. This is just the kind of toxic feedback that plays on your self-confidence and makes it harder to get up and do it all again.

You will need to make a judgement call on either or both of these scenarios at some time in your presenting career.

AUDIENCE REACTION

If the members of the audience laugh in the right places, applaud wildly when you finish and carry you shoulder high from the stage, cheering loudly along the way, you can be pretty sure you've done OK.

A positive audience reaction tells its own story, but even if this doesn't happen, it might not be that those in the audience don't like you. I have delivered the same speech, twice in one week, to different audiences and had completely different reactions. First time, you would have thought I was Bill Clinton crossed with Jerry Seinfeld, whereas during the second address there was utter silence. What was really frustrating about this was after the second address, during the coffee break, half a dozen different people approached me and said how much they had enjoyed what I had done. Tempted as I was to say 'Well next time, why don't you let your face show it?', I simply thanked them instead and concluded just because they don't look like they love you, doesn't mean that they hate you. A good lesson, that one.

FUTURE BOOKINGS

Often you will find that speaking as an invited guest at an event leads to being approached to speak at others in the future. If this happens you can be sure you must have put on a good performance. At some point, people will be happy to pay you for your services and when that day comes, you realize you have arrived as a speaker.

With this in mind, always have some business cards to hand or some way people can contact you. Try not to get drawn into negotiation there and then. It is much better to do this away from the noise of the crowd, so suggest instead that you meet, or telephone in the next day or so.

FORMAL FEEDBACK

I've highlighted the fact that at many events and conferences, there will be a written evaluation form for delegates to complete. Try using the advanced techniques discussed to improve the quality of this, but at the very least you can be sure of getting a set of scores to reflect upon. There is usually a space for comments too although usually only a small percentage of delegates fill these in.

Whatever the outturn of the feedback, treat it with caution. We've recognized that at the end of a long day, most delegates want to race for the car and hit the road homewards. They're often not very concerned with 'giving their feedback', so you should judge the scores with this in mind.

This is why I have said we are always drawn to the most negative end of the spectrum. If 199 delegates give you 10 out of 10, you will focus on the one remaining who scored you at 4. I know speakers who gave up looking through the forms years ago!

Balance your approach here, don't ignore negative comments altogether or this will result in the sort of arrogance which will stop you improving, but keep a sense of proportion: it's unlikely we will engage with all the people all of the time.

Take all the methods I've suggested for measuring your performance and begin to track them over time, then you start to build up a much more accurate picture of just how good a presenter you are.

To help you formalize and track your progress, the presentation analysis grid in Table 20.1 sets out some headings and asks you to fill in your marks, add comments and consider what you will do next. A couple of the fields are filled in to give you an idea of what is required.

Table 20.1 Presentation analysis grid

Skill set	Marks out of 10	Comments	What next?
Content			
Confidence	6	*Bit shaky at the start, but OK after that.*	*Take my time. Deep breath before I begin.*
Presence/Charisma			
Conviction/Passion			
Voice			
Audience handling			
Resilience	7	*Q & A went well. Didn't panic over minor details.*	*Practise keeping calm under pressure*
Overall performance			

Activity

Use your diary or a wall planner to map out some milestones. Make the goals personal to you and keep them realistic, then decide when you wish to reach each stage by and chart your progress. You might consider goals such as 'Write 10 minutes on communication skills', 'Develop a PowerPoint template' or 'Deliver a short presentation without notes'.

SUMMARY

- Make time for personal reflection following each presentation and be honest about how your performance went.

- Take into account the views of as wide a group of people as possible when assessing your performance.

- Audience reaction is a great test for success. Did the audience enjoy it? Balance this with what people actually say afterwards.

- Take the positives out of the feedback forms and try to be objective about any negative comment.

- When you have assimilated all your measures of success, think about how you could be better next time.

WHAT NEXT?

As far as I can see, you're pretty much ready to take the stage. Whatever your past experience has been of presenting, I hope some of the ideas outlined in this book are of positive benefit. Sometimes the best learning is about simply avoiding the mistakes. I hope you manage that too.

For some food for thought about where to take your presentation skills next, I have put together some notes to suggest a possible way forward.

BEYOND BEST PRACTICE

In a previous book that I co-authored with Professor Cary L Cooper, called *Business and the Beautiful Game* (published by Kogan Page) we considered what those involved in the commercial sector could learn from examining the world of soccer. Underpinning this idea was the thought that there was something beyond best practice. It seemed that the mantra of the 1990s that urged us to seek out the best in our own industry had its limitations. Chase the leaders and by the time you get to where they are, they will have moved on. Therefore, we theorized that by looking at other aspects of our lives, we might be able to translate some of the lessons learned into our own environment.

The same is true, I believe, of presentation skills, and an arena where we can draw on hard-won experience is live theatre. Given that the best way to improve our presentation skills is to practise, practise, practise, joining a local theatrical society and having the opportunity to appear on stage is a great way to increase your personal 'flying hours'. Perhaps one of the added benefits of this is that it allows the opportunity to try things out behind the mask of the character you are playing. You will also have been given a script, meaning the writing phase has been done for you!

PROJECTION

Acting has its roots far away in the past, before all the technology we now take for granted had been invented. Often this was combined with the task of playing to a large audience, some of whom would inevitably be a long way from the stage. Maybe this is why 'acting' necessitates being 'larger than life'. Gestures are bigger, the voice is used in a grander fashion and facial expressions are more pronounced. How else would the watching public get a sense of what the cast is attempting to portray? Go too far and there is a risk of 'hamming it up', but the mistake that lots of amateur actors and, coincidentally, presenters make is that they fail to 'act up' enough. The stage (whether theatrical or commercial) requires you to be bigger than normal in order to convey your message.

A great way of illustrating this is to watch yourself on video. Do you really look as if you are passionate when you hit the critical bit of your speech? Is your emotion conveyed right to the back of the room? Unless you are a 'natural', it is unlikely. The way we speak needs to be more pronounced. We have to articulate our words more clearly than normal; pauses that might seem like a lifetime when you are standing up there shrink to a mere beat when you reflect back on them.

I am not advocating here that you turn yourself into some kind of a parody of Shakespearean grandeur, or bellow and gesticulate so wildly that you put fear into the first three rows of audience members, but if you 'turn it up' by a notch or two you will be amazed how much more convincing you look and sound.

TOOLS OF THE TRADE

Costume, props, lighting and make-up are the stock-in-trade of the professional theatre actor. And since you ask, no, I am not suggesting you smear on the greasepaint before presenting the latest sales figures to the board, but instead consider what all of this is trying to achieve.

Enhancing the way you look, sound and act are all part of being a great speaker. What we wear becomes part of the representation of what we are seeking to put across. The 'staging' of the event is vitally important. Who is in charge of lighting and sound? If you cannot be heard, or even worse seen, because dimming the lights to enhance the PowerPoint has left you in semi-darkness, it will unsettle your audience.

When it comes to props, these are as legitimate on the business or social stage as they are in the theatre. Of course they have to be relevant, well chosen to add weight to your point and visible. Used correctly they can be a powerful addition to your message. Generally speaking, with a big audience, large props are necessary so everyone can clearly see what you are talking about, but there are exceptions. I witnessed a presenter who was trying to make a point about customer service at a top hotel. He illustrated it by holding up a tiny piece of paper, forcing his audience to lean forward to get a better view. He went on to say the note contained the guest's name, which had been helpfully copied from the luggage label and written by the taxi driver who picked the guest up from the airport. The note was passed to each employee at the hotel, who was then able to greet the guest by name as he or she arrived.

CHARACTER

Mostly the character up there is you, or at least a slightly exaggerated version, which means being true to yourself, so people still recognize you during the post-presentation reception. However, I have seen some neat tricks pulled off by using 'character'. I once witnessed a highly effective sales rally, where the presenter had dressed as an army colonel, complete with swagger stick and literally rallied his 'troops' (the sales team) by outlining in army parlance the 'battle' ahead. Against the odds, against the competition and in the spirit of true teamwork; brilliant if you can pull it off.

By the same token, many professional presenters illustrate their stories by 'becoming' the characters in them. A friend of mine in education 'plays out' a conversation between a teacher and an early years student, by physically taking up the different positions of each and changing voice from 'authoritative' to 'squeaky'. It's funny, endearing and makes his point in a very powerful way.

These are, of course, extremes and they take practice, skill and a high degree of courage to achieve, but they make the point that 'characterization' is important. It is worth noting here, as I do elsewhere, the bigger the performance, the greater the risk. The truth is that it is much more likely you will look like an idiot if you attempt this kind of outrageous behaviour and don't manage to pull it off. What counterbalances the risk though is if you can deliver well, under such circumstances, people will remember it for a long time to come. For example, the performance with the presenter as an army colonel was something I witnessed 20 years ago and I am still talking about it now!

FREQUENCY

Most actors who rehearse for the theatre get multiple chances to deliver their script. Talk to some at the end of a long run and they will tell you how much easier it became as time went by. There is a lesson here about the difference between rehearsal and perform-ance. Just as with sports stars, who might practise on the training ground, it is never the same when you hit the field of play. In front of a live audience, you will find out whether your one-liners are funny or not, you will discover what it is that engages people – and often it will not be the parts you thought would engage them – and you will come to understand what they want more of and, critically, what they would like less of. All of this might not mean changing the content, but the way you deliver it, the running order, how your words blend with the visuals or the pauses you take. Just as in acting.

FAMILIARITY

Linked to frequency is the key element of familiarity. The better acquainted you become with a presentation, the more at ease you are in delivering it. No longer are you worried about 'forgetting your lines', instead you can start to consider the other elements that will add weight to what you are saying. The pace and tone of your delivery, where you place your emphasis, how you use your passion – all these things are important in bringing the words to life.

Actors talk about 'finding the character'. What they mean is that beyond the lines they need to learn there will be traits like an accent, a lisp, a way of standing and moving around – all the elements that are the 'essence' of who they are playing. None of this can be achieved until they are 100 per cent comfortable with the script, having learned it by heart. I am not advocating you have to be able to deliver your speech verbatim, from a script you have written, but simply saying your ability to 'enhance' the words will be much improved once you are familiar with the content.

If you don't see yourself as a budding actor, you might not share my enthusiasm for theatre as a means of improving presentation skills. However, there are some excellent learning points we can all draw from theatre and you would be amazed at the number of professional presenters who 'trod the boards' at some point in their past life.

AND FINALLY...

I hope some of this advice proves to be useful. Even if it just helps to get you up on the stage in the first place then it is mission accomplished, because once you're there, I promise you, you will be able to handle it.

Think back to what I said at the start – this book is called *Develop Your Presentation Skills* and in the final analysis, it is all about you – that is who the audience has come to see.

Be yourself, be as well rehearsed as you possibly can and be prepared for the audience to love you. Oh, and one other thing, as they say in all the most fashionable restaurants these days: Enjoy!

9 780749 467029